Decoding the Court: Legal Data Insights from the Supreme Court of Canada

This edited collection combines state-of-the-art legal data analytics with in-depth doctrinal analysis to study the Supreme Court of Canada (SCC), Canada's top court. A data analytics perspective adds new dimensions to the study of courts and their case law. It renders legal analysis scalable, making it possible to investigate thousands of judicial decisions, adding new breadth and depth. It also enables researchers to combine doctrinal questions about how the law evolves with institutional questions about how courts operate, shedding new light on how law works in practice. By applying a range of methods to study the content of SCC decisions, this work bridges the gap between qualitative and quantitative research. Demonstrating how new analytical perspectives can generate new insights about the Supreme Court, an institution which is closely studied by scholars both within and outside Canada, the book will be essential reading for legal scholars and political scientists, particularly those working in public law and in empirical legal studies.

Wolfgang Alschner is Associate Professor at the University of Ottawa, where he leads the Legal Technology Lab.

Vanessa MacDonnell is Associate Professor at the University of Ottawa Faculty of Law and Co-Director of the uOttawa Public Law Centre.

Carissima Mathen is Full Professor at the University of Ottawa Faculty of Law, Canada.

Decoding the Court: Legal Data Insights from the Supreme Court of Canada

Edited by
Wolfgang Alschner, Vanessa
MacDonnell and Carissima Mathen

Routledge
Taylor & Francis Group
LONDON AND NEW YORK

First published 2024
by Routledge
4 Park Square, Milton Park, Abingdon, Oxon OX14 4RN

and by Routledge
605 Third Avenue, New York, NY 10158

Routledge is an imprint of the Taylor & Francis Group, an informa business

British Library Cataloguing-in-Publication Data
A catalogue record for this book is available from the British Library

Library of Congress Cataloging-in-Publication Data
Names: Alschner, Wolfgang, editor. | MacDonnell, Vanessa, editor. | Mathen, Carissima, editor.
Title: Decoding the court : legal data insights from the Supreme Court of Canada / edited by Wolfgang Alschner, Vanessa MacDonnell, and Carissima Mathen.
Identifiers: LCCN 2023051568 (print) | LCCN 2023051569 (ebook) | ISBN 9781032245256 (hardback) | ISBN 9781032245270 (paperback) | ISBN 9781003279112 (ebook)
Subjects: LCSH: Canada. Supreme Court. | Separation of powers–Canada. | Judicial process–Canada. | Justice, Administration of–Canada. | Courts–Canada.
Classification: LCC KE8244 .D43 2024 (print) | LCC KE8244 (ebook) | DDC 347.71/035–dc23/eng/20231108
LC record available at https://lccn.loc.gov/2023051568
LC ebook record available at https://lccn.loc.gov/2023051569

ISBN: 978-1-032-24525-6 (hbk)
ISBN: 978-1-032-24527-0 (pbk)
ISBN: 978-1-003-27911-2 (ebk)

DOI: 10.4324/9781003279112

Typeset in Galliard
by Deanta Global Publishing Services, Chennai, India

The Open Access version of this book was funded by Social Sciences and Humanities Research Council of Canada

Contents

Contributors

Wolfgang Alschner: Associate Professor at the Common Law Section, University of Ottawa, co-director of the University of Ottawa Legal Tech Lab, specializing in international economic law and the computational analysis of law.

Vanessa MacDonnell: Associate Professor at the Common Law Section, University of Ottawa, co-director of the University of Ottawa Public Law Centre, researching Canadian constitutional law, constitutional theory, and criminal law.

Carissima Mathen: Full Professor of Law at the Common Law Section, University of Ottawa, award-winning author and researcher in Canadian constitutional and criminal law.

Keenan MacNeal: Graduate of the English JD program of the Common Law Section, University of Ottawa.

Stephen Bindman: Visiting Professor at the Common Law Section, University of Ottawa, Former Senior Advisor in the Policy Sector of the Department of Justice Canada.

Kelley Humber: Graduate of the English JD program of the Common Law Section, University of Ottawa.

Terry Skolnik: Associate Professor (tenured) at the University of Ottawa, Faculty of Law, Civil Law Section, and co-director of the University of Ottawa Public Law Centre.

Paul-Erik Veel: Partner at Lenczner Slaght with expertise in class actions, competition law, and intellectual property litigation.

Katie Glowach: Associate at Lenczner Slaght, specializing in commercial litigation, public law, and professional liability matters.

Isabelle St-Hilaire: DPhil student at the University of Oxford.

Jena McGill: Associate Professor at the Common Law Section, University of Ottawa, researching Canadian constitutional law, gender and sexuality, and legal technology to promote access to justice.

Amy Salyzyn: Associate Professor at the Common Law Section, University of Ottawa, focusing on legal ethics, gender and the law, law and technology, and civil justice reform.

Introduction

Wolfgang Alschner, Vanessa MacDonnell, and Carissima Mathen

Apex courts and the impactful decisions they render captivate the attention of society. They are a favourite topic of scholars in fields ranging from law to political science, are subject to constant media coverage, and shape the public's perception of law, justice, and the state like few other institutions. Yet how much do we really know about these ultimate arbiters of justice? For every sentence that legal scholars dissect under the microscope of doctrinal analysis, innumerable others are merely skimmed. For every landmark precedent that enters the law school curriculum, there are thousands of cases that are never mentioned. Despite the tremendous scrutiny, much of what apex courts do escapes our collective attention.

The Supreme Court of Canada is a case in point. Over 11,000 decisions have been rendered by the Court since 1885. These decisions, in turn, have been cited by more than 1,110,000 other court decisions. This amount of legal information is too vast for even the most dedicated scholar to process. That, however, creates problems. How comprehensive can our analysis be if we are ever only looking at parts of a larger whole?[1] What do we miss when we rely exclusively on traditional doctrinal methods? And, conversely, what could we see and learn if we were able to study apex courts and their decisions more systematically?

This book seeks to expand our gaze to include the whole as well as the parts. Doing so requires new tools. The microscope of traditional legal analysis cannot be used to study law from 30,000 feet, nor does it easily permit controlled study of individual legal phenomena. For that, we must turn to techniques that treat law as data. These research techniques cover a wide spectrum, from computer-assisted tools known variously as "legal data science",[2] "digital humanities",[3] "computational legal

---

1 See generally William Baude, Adam Chilton, and Anup Malani, "Making Doctrinal Work More Rigorous: Lessons from Systematic Reviews" (2017) 84 Chic L Rev 37.
2 See the University of Ottawa's Legal Text Mining Lab, *Data Science for Lawyers*, online: www.datascienceforlawyers.org.
3 Nina Varsava, "Computational Legal Studies, Digital Humanities, and Textual Analysis" in Ryan Whalen, ed., *Computational Legal Studies* (Cheltenham: Edward Elgar Publishing,

DOI: 10.4324/9781003279112-1

studies",[4] or "quantitative methods",[5] to manual data collection efforts, including systematic content and doctrinal analyses and descriptive statistics. What these approaches have in common is that they put systematic data gathering and analysis centre stage, and use these legal data insights to augment and complement traditional doctrinal studies. As we will show throughout this book, combining data science with doctrinal and normative analyses to study the Supreme Court of Canada systematically over time can generate new insights into core questions of interest to legal scholars, political scientists, and practitioners and inform the study of apex courts more generally.

I.1 Law as Data

A growing body of scholarship has begun to understand *law* as *data*.[6] Data are not only tabulated numbers in a spreadsheet; text is a form of data too. That makes law, which consists primarily of large amounts of text, an ideal field for the application of law-as-data tools. These tools build on lawyers' long-standing practice of investigating legal texts in depth. But while scholars have traditionally engaged with legal sources through textual interpretation and close reading alone, lawyers can also benefit from a "distant reading" of texts.[7]

Such a "distant reading" of law is not new. In the 1980s, law professor Harold Spaeth began systematically classifying US Supreme Court decisions.[8] However, the absence of systematic content analysis training in law schools limited the adoption of such approaches to a small cohort of empirically inclined legal scholars. The need for laborious and costly manual analysis has discouraged the use of these approaches or confined them to smaller sets, samples, or variables. Two developments have begun to change this. First, the growing interest in the empirical and interdisciplinary analysis of law is beginning to bridge the divide between

---

2020), https://www.elgaronline.com/view/edcoll/9781788977449/9781788977449 .00007.xml (accessed July 20, 2022).

4 Ryan Whalen, ed., *Computational Legal Studies: The Promise and Challenge of Data-Driven Research* (Cheltenham: Edward Elgar Publishing, 2020).

5 Urška Šadl and Henrik Palmer Olsen, "Can Quantitative Methods Complement Doctrinal Legal Studies? Using Citation Network and Corpus Linguistic Analysis to Understand International Courts" (2017) 30 Leiden J Intl L 327.

6 Livermore, Michael, and Daniel Rockmore, eds. *Law as Data: Computation, Text, and the Future of Legal Analysis* (San Francisco: SFI Press, 2019).

7 Wolfgang Alschner, "The Computational Analysis of International Law" in Rossana Deplano and Nicholas Tsagourias, eds, *Research Methods in International Law: A Handbook* (Cheltenham: Edward Elgar, 2021).

8 Harold J. Spaeth and Saul Brenner, *Studies in U.S. Supreme Court Behavior* (New York: Garland Publishing, 1990).

quantitative and doctrinal scholarship, and has raised awareness of the complementary nature of these approaches. Second, new technologies have radically decreased the costs of conducting large-scale analyses and broadened the toolbox of researchers as technology is increasingly doing the heavy lifting.

Three computer-assisted tools are particularly promising for studying law as data. First, natural language processing (NLP) treats text as data. Documents are "processed" by algorithms rather than read by humans. NLP regroups a broad array of techniques that range from relatively simple rule-based pattern-matching algorithms, so-called regular expressions, which we use extensively in this book, to more complex statistical modelling of texts. Second, machine learning, a form of artificial intelligence, learns the relationship between input and output. Machine learning is useful, for example, in predicting the outcome of judicial decisions based on descriptions or content features of a case. Finally, network analysis is a prominent data science technique that displays relationships, such as citations of judicial decisions, as a network. The commonality between these different techniques is that they (1) treat legal information as data, (2) are usually implemented in a programming environment, and (3) are scalable, meaning they can efficiently investigate large collections of text.

Together, these methods create new scope, scale, and depth for empirical, doctrinal, and institutional analysis of law. First, data science tools render empirical analysis more accessible, affordable, and adaptive, which broadens its possible uses. A few lines of computer code can generate a bird's-eye view of courts and their case law that reveals patterns or trends over time, but that also allows researchers to zoom in to study these structures in depth. Second, both manual and computer-assisted studies of decisions complement doctrinal research. The American law scholar Lawrence Friedman once noted that "Qualitative analysis without quantitative evidence tend[s] to be entertaining anecdotes; quantitative analysis without qualitative data is often blind".[9] In that spirit, it is the combination of the qualitative and quantitative, the distant and close reading, the micro and macro level, that can be most revealing. As we will elaborate throughout the book, we believe that particularly rich insights can be gained when we zoom out as well as zoom in to study decisions in detail but also in context. Finally, distant reading techniques provide new ways to study how courts operate, shedding new light on how law works in practice. They allow engagement with political and normative debates surrounding courts, based on a sound empirical footing.

---

9 Quoted in Sergio Puig, "Network Analysis and the Sociology of International Law" in Moshe Hirsch and Andrew Lang, eds, *Research Handbook on the Sociology of International Law* (Cheltenham: Edward Elgar, 2018), 319, 332.

In this Introduction, we set up the discussion that follows and highlight from the outset the challenges of doing this work as a multi-disciplinary research team composed of people who bring fundamentally different skills to the task of investigating and synthesizing judicial decisions. In undertaking the project, we were keenly aware of how quickly the landscape is shifting, and that this book represents a moment in time in the story of integrating legal data insights into the study of apex courts.

I.2 Introducing the Supreme Court

This book employs a variety of techniques to study core questions about the Supreme Court of Canada. As a court of final appeal, the Supreme Court occupies a rarified position. It identifies and shapes the rules by which people live, and by which state institutions make decisions and exercise power. It settles disputes and provides advice in every area of law, from commercial transactions, environmental regulation, and Indigenous land claims to criminal procedure. It affects the relationships between orders of government; guides the work of lower courts and administrative agencies; formulates constitutional principles; and renders judgments that affect the lives of tens of millions of people. The Court's work is multi-variate: dependent upon dozens of inputs, factors, and facts, and expressed through sophisticated and occasionally dense legal analysis.

In addition to deciding cases and offering advisory opinions, the Supreme Court grants leave to parties to intervene and to present evidence; decides who may make oral submissions (and for how long); and sets its own rules and procedures. A focus on the Court's appellate function cannot therefore produce a complete picture of its work. Nonetheless, its appellate judgments and advisory opinions are the most important components of its work, and are thus an appropriate basis upon which to focus empirical study. Thus, with some exceptions, the chapters that follow focus on instances of complex reasoning by which the Court has arrived at a decision point. We aim to show how empirical approaches can assist people in understanding the institution, and to show the relationship between those decisions and the Court as an institution.

I.3 Continuing a Methodological Conversation

The book's methodological approach is supported by a small but significant body of scholarship that uses empirical approaches to investigate the work of apex courts. Empirical work on the Supreme Court of Canada (SCC) has tended to be dominated by political scientists, and has prioritized institutional aspects, such as the ideological tendencies of Supreme

Court judges or authorship of Supreme Court decisions.[10] Political scientists Ostberg and Wetstein, as well as Songer, have explored the ideological leanings of SCC justices, and modelled the justices' decision-making by examining their voting behaviour, among other things.[11] McCormick's scholarship combines data on dissents and citation patterns to study the court's normative evolution.[12]

Legal research on the Supreme Court using empirical or data science techniques has been limited, and has often mirrored the preoccupations and methods of political scientists. For example, Alarie and Green have used the hand-coding of variables combined with traditional statistical analysis to investigate institutional questions, such as ideological tendencies among SCC justices, the importance of ideology in the acceptance of applications for leave, and the role of interveners.[13]

To the best of our knowledge, legal scholarship applying computer science methods such as natural language processing or network analysis to the SCC remains rare, and there are no monograph-length treatments of this topic. In 2013, Neale conducted a large-scale citation analysis of Canadian courts, including the Supreme Court of Canada.[14] The study is insightful from a methodological perspective, discussing, for example, different network analysis measures to model precedential authority; however, it does not engage in a significant way with either the Supreme Court as an institution or its case law. Work by Bodwin et al. uses natural language processing to investigate the authorship of Supreme Court decisions, finding that clerks increasingly co-draft Supreme Court decisions with the judges for whom they work.[15]

10 Macfarlane, Emmett. *Governing from the Bench: The Supreme Court of Canada and the Judicial Role* (Vancouver: UBC Press, 2013).

11 Ostberg, C. L., and Matthew E. Wetstein. *Attitudinal Decision Making in the Supreme Court of Canada*. Law and Society (Vancouver: UBC Press, 2007). Ostberg, C. L., and Matthew E. Wetstein. *Value Change in the Supreme Court of Canada* (Toronto: University of Toronto Press, 2017). Songer, Donald R. *The Transformation of the Supreme Court of Canada an Empirical Examination* (Toronto: University of Toronto Press, 2008). Songer, Donald R. *Law, Ideology, and Collegiality Judicial Behaviour in the Supreme Court of Canada* (Montréal: McGill-Queen's University Press, 2012).

12 McCormick, Peter J. *The End of the Charter Revolution: Looking Back from the New Normal* (Toronto: University of Toronto Press Higher Education, 2014).

13 Benjamin Alarie and Andrew Green, "Charter Decisions in the McLachlin Era: Consensus and Ideology at the Supreme Court of Canada" (2009) 47:1 Supreme Court Law Rev Osgoode's Annu Const Cases Conf,; Benjamin Alarie and Andrew Green, "Interventions at the Supreme Court of Canada: Accuracy, Affiliation, and Acceptance" (2010) 48 Osgoode Hall Law J 30.

14 Thom Neale, "Citation Analysis of Canadian Case Law" (2013) 1: 1 Data Organization and Legal Informatics 1.

15 Bodwin, Kelly, Jeffrey S Rosenthal, and Albert H Yoon. "Opinion Writing and Authorship on the Supreme Court of Canada." 63 University of Toronto Law Journal 159.

Only very recently have doctrinal and legal institutional studies of the Canadian Supreme Court taken a more data-driven stance. A 2017 study by Murchison manually coded almost 300 Supreme Court cases on the Charter to measure different dimensions of judicial activism.[16] A 2022 article by Bogach, Opolsky, and Veel relied on a new hand-coded database of Supreme Court of Canada decisions to track the use of from-the-bench decisions. Both studies carefully combine quantitative analysis to identify larger trends with doctrinal case studies to evaluate normative implications.[17] Such studies promise new and important insights. At the same time, the labour-intensiveness of the manual analysis creates significant upfront costs.

The advent of more powerful computational approaches presents an important shift in context, as the international scholarship demonstrates. For example, Fowler et al. have used data science techniques to trace the use of precedent by the United States Supreme Court (SCOTUS) in more than 30,000 majority opinions, finding, among other things, that overruled decisions continue to be cited and that landmark decisions sometimes take years to be recognized as such.[18] European law scholars have also used data science to challenge textbook accounts of what counts as the system's most influential cases, and have blurred the divide between civil law and common law systems when it comes to precedent.[19] Using the European Court of Human Rights as a case study, scholars relied on a natural language processing technique called topic modelling to track how judicial principles have evolved across decades of case law.[20] Finally, these techniques have been harnessed to investigate how courts frame their decisions. Busch and Pelc, for example, find that adjudicators at the World Trade Organization use more emotional language when deciding politically controversial issues.[21] In short, both nationally and

16 Melanie Murchison, "Making Numbers Count: An Empirical Analysis of 'Judicial Activism' in Canada" (2017) 40 Man LJ (Robson Crim) 423.

17 Alex Bogach, Jeremy Opolsky, and Paul-Erik Veel, "The Supreme Court of Canada's From-the-Bench Decisions" (2022) 106 Supreme Court Law Review, 2ⁿᵈ Series.

18 James H. Fowler et al., "Network Analysis and the Law: Measuring the Legal Importance of Precedents at the U.S. Supreme Court" (2007) 15 Political Analysis 324.

19 Mattias Derlén and Johan Lindholm, "Goodbye van Gend En Loos, Hello Bosman? Using Network Analysis to Measure the Importance of Individual CJEU Judgments" (2014) 20 European LJ 667.

20 Panagis, Yannis, Martin Lolle Christensen, and Urška Šadl. "On Top of Topics: Leveraging Topic Modeling to Study the Dynamic Case-Law of International Courts of Law." In *Legal Knowledge and Information Systems*, edited by Floris Bex. Frontiers in Artificial Intelligence and Applications. IOS Press, 2016.

21 Marc L. Busch and Krzysztof J. Pelc, "Words Matter: How WTO Rulings Handle Controversy" (2019) International Studies Quarterly, online: https://academic.oup.com/isq/advance-article/doi/10.1093/isq/sqz025/5499120 (accessed July 19, 2019).

internationally and across diverse areas of laws, scholars have begun to answer legal questions using data science methods.

This book combines quantitative and doctrinal insights, and directs its attention to both jurisprudential and institutional questions; however, it relies more on programming than on manual analysis. To be sure, manual work remains crucial at the front end, when designing code and selecting algorithms, as well as at the back end, when validating and interpreting results. The greater reliance on computation rather than manual counting has two advantages, though. First, it permits almost costless rerunning of the analysis when new data comes in, allowing for a dynamic updating of results over time. Second, it opens the door to new types of analysis that we showcase in this book, from the creation of complex citation networks to the prediction of judicial decisions. With the advent of large language models that are more powerful when it comes to processing texts and new interfaces, like chatbots that can execute code in a conversational setting, we are convinced that as these tools become more accessible, legal researchers will increasingly treat text as data.

At the same time, data science, empirical analysis, and doctrinal scholarship can interact with and enrich each other in a wide range of ways. Lawyers do not have to become social scientists or computer programmers to produce empirically grounded scholarship or to use systematic data gathering to support their doctrinal argumentation. Indeed, the contributions in this book occupy a broad spectrum between doctrinal analysis supported by systematic, but manual, data analysis to state-of-the-art network analysis and machine learning applications that would have been impossible to conduct without computer programming.

This book thereby seeks to continue a methodological conversation that eschews traditional distinctions between doctrinal and empirical or qualitative and quantitative research, and fully embraces a mixed-methods approach. It is also, for this reason, more resistant to some of the critiques that tend to be raised in response to the use of quantitative methods to study courts and court decisions. For example, it is sometimes suggested that quantitative analysis reveals relatively little about the work of courts; that the mere "counting" of cases does not materially advance our understanding of the institution and can sometimes even be misleading in its lack of context. The mixed-methods approach we adopt here brings together the benefits of empirical and doctrinal analyses to develop a more complex picture of the Supreme Court as an institution. The use of data science techniques permits certain trends in the jurisprudence to be investigated through comprehensive and systematic analysis. Other parts of the project seek to pair empirical findings with a deep understanding of the Court's history, context, practices, and doctrine. This marriage of methods, and the dialectic between them, results in a more nuanced set of research findings.

I.4 Pushing the Boundaries

Interdisciplinary collaboration that seeks to pair legal research questions with the appropriate social science or computer science methods is challenging, but it has the potential to push the boundaries of legal scholarship in new directions in at least two ways. First, it facilitates the exploration of questions that long seemed out of reach for legal researchers. Scholars of the Supreme Court and of Canadian constitutional law tend to have an intuitive sense of the types of research questions that are worth pursuing, and instincts about the likely answers to those questions. This might include, for example, views about particular judges' propensity to dissent, the importance of particular precedents, or features of a case that render it more likely that leave to appeal will be granted by the Court. Yet scholars typically lack the skills to investigate these questions at scale. Legal data scientists, for their part, have expertise in the range of tools available for pursuing particular research questions, a sense of which tools are best suited to answering which research questions, and opinions about how different tools can be paired to further deepen the research. Once legal questions are matched with data science methods – a challenging alignment problem in its own right – legal trends that were previously out of reach become accessible. Dissent patterns can be tracked and evaluated, the importance of a precedent quantified, and the determinants of leave to appeal applications revealed. Implicit assumptions are explicitly tested, validated, or falsified, and hunches are turned into insights and knowledge.

Second, sometimes trends or patterns in the jurisprudence only become obvious because of the data analysis itself. Data scientists have called this "letting data speak for itself".[22] In this case, the data is not confirming instinct, but is rather surfacing trends that were not previously visible. For this reason, it is not enough to structure a project around the intuitions of scholars studying the Court and its jurisprudence. The researcher must also be open to the story that the data is telling. For doctrinal scholars in particular, this requires that the researcher approach legal analysis somewhat differently than they might otherwise. It requires greater openness to trial and error; to pursuing a research avenue and concluding that it turns up nothing, or something unexpected; and to interrogating the received wisdom about an institution they feel they know very well.

Finally, it is worth noting that a project of this type can sometimes prove confronting for researchers, regardless of their background and

22 Viktor Mayer-Schönberger and Kenneth Cukier, *Big Data: A Revolution That Will Transform How We Live, Work, and Think*, reprint edition (Boston, MA: Eamon Dolan/Mariner Books, 2014).

expertise. The study of the Supreme Court using a mixed-methods approach invariably forces the researcher to accept gaps in their knowledge of law and legal institutions, and to recognize that their approach to studying the institution is only one approach among others, each of which has its strengths and weaknesses.

The core of our project – merging the expertise of empirical and doctrinal legal scholars – recognizes the benefits and risks of a data-driven approach. Data is important, critical even, but it is not everything. Data alone cannot provide nearly the same level of insight as mediating that data through subject-matter expertise. As Andrea Jones-Rooy put it, "Data is a necessary ingredient in discovery, but you need a human to select it, shape it, and then turn it into an insight".[23] In aligning empirical methods and doctrinal reasoning, it became clear to us how much of the subsequent analysis relied on multiple, interlocking factors which go beyond those tools. It is one thing to formulate questions and then, through the application of data science to a dataset, generate results. It is another thing to determine, in the case of this work specifically, what conclusions those results support about an institution like the Supreme Court.

I.5 The Book

The volume opens with a chapter by Wolfgang Alschner and Keenan Macneal introducing the Supreme Court of Canada dataset created for this book. The authors then present the book's three research streams – (1) the evolution of the Court, (2) cleavages on the Court, and (3) changing judicial practice – and use the dataset to canvass developments under each stream. To map the Court's evolution as an institution, Alschner and Macneal employ citation analysis to identify the Court's landmark rulings. Under cleavages, they examine divisions along gender lines, and trace the growing influence of women judges on the Supreme Court through an analysis of the proportion of the judgments they author, the frequency with which they join a concurrence or a dissent, and the type of language they use in their decisions. Finally, the authors explore the Court's evolving practices, including the phenomenon of the Supreme Court hearing fewer cases over time, but issuing longer judgments in those cases. Aside from providing original insights about the Court, the chapter also sets the stage for subsequent chapters that zoom in on specific research questions under each stream.

---

23 Andrea Jones-Rooy, "I'm a data scientist who is skeptical about data," Blog Post, Quartz, 24 July 2019: https://qz.com/1664575/is-data-science-legit (accessed 2 September 2023).

Vanessa MacDonnell and Keenan Macneal's chapter kicks off the research stream on the evolving Court. It uses systematic doctrinal analysis to study the evolution of Canada's separation of powers doctrine, demonstrating how data science can both complement and enhance traditional research. There have long been conflicting views about the salience of the separation of powers as a constitutional principle in Canada. MacDonnell and Macneal's research finds that the separation of powers is indeed an important constitutional principle; in fact, references to the principle appear to be on the rise in the Supreme Court's jurisprudence. They also find that a subset of judges has led this trend, and in particular, that Justice Karakatsanis has emerged as the intellectual leader in the separation of powers jurisprudence. While the Court appears to have settled on the basic meaning of the doctrine, however, it has often been divided on how that doctrine applies in concrete cases. This has generated several sets of dissenting reasons on separation of powers issues.

In Chapter 3, Wolfgang Alschner and Isabelle St-Hilaire continue the study of the Court's evolution by looking at the rise and fall of Supreme Court precedents over time. They employ both network analysis and natural language processing to develop a more fine-grained account of the influence of individual precedents than simple citation counts would permit. Alschner and St-Hilaire identify four "precedential archetypes" that appear in the data. The first is "the eternal star", by which they mean a case that has maintained a high authority score over a long period of time. The second is "the forgotten pioneer", which is a case that once played a central role in the Court's jurisprudence, but was later overtaken by newer precedents. The third is "the central focal point", which is a case that is highly salient across a range of subject areas, and the final archetype is the "niche anchor", which is a case that has a high authority score but that is cited within a more limited area of the law. Alschner and St-Hilaire argue that these archetypes can help scholars develop a more refined understanding of the life cycle of a precedent and the nature of its authority.

Turning to cleavages on the Court, in Chapter 4, Carissima Mathen, Stephen Bindman, Kelley Humber, and Keenan Macneal use legal data analytics to explore the phenomenon of disagreement in the Supreme Court's judgments. They explain that a focus on a broad understanding of "disagreement" helps illuminate aspects of the Supreme Court's practices in ways that a focus on dissent alone cannot. Their research demonstrates that the Court's post-1982 jurisprudence is defined by two "distinct periods of fracturing": the first, which covers the period from the late 1980s to the mid-1990s, was driven by concurrences, while the second, covering the period from 2015 to the present, has been driven by dissents. In the most recent period, the dissenting profile of Justice Côté is a particular outlier.

In Chapter 5, Terry Skolnik and Keenan Macneal use descriptive statistics to examine the Supreme Court's citation of secondary sources in private law cases. They compare the Court's practices in Quebec cases, in which private law disputes are governed by civil law, with those in non-Quebec cases, in which they are governed by common law. They note that although the Court is formally bilingual and bijural, the Court cites French sources more often in Quebec private law cases, and English sources more often in private law cases from jurisdictions outside of Quebec. They also find that bilingual sources are cited more frequently in Quebec cases than in non-Quebec cases. Their research suggests that academic sources written in English may not be contributing as much as they could to the development of civil law, and that the same is true of French sources in respect of common law.

In the last part of the book, dedicated to judicial practice, Paul-Erik Veel and Katie Glowach provide an overview of the Supreme Court of Canada Leave Project, an innovative new machine learning platform that predicts which cases are most likely to be granted leave by the Supreme Court of Canada. As Veel and Glowach note, only a small fraction of cases for which leave to appeal is sought are ultimately heard by the Supreme Court of Canada (approximately 10% on average). The factors that influence the granting of leave are therefore matters of great interest for litigants and counsel, as is the ability to predict the likelihood of success in seeking leave. Veel and Glowach's research shows that certain factors appear to increase the likelihood of a case being granted leave, such as a case being overturned on appeal and a dissent in the Court of Appeal. Their research also shows that certain factors are *not* more likely to lead to a case being granted leave, including a case being concerned with an area of law, such as constitutional law, that is viewed as highly important.

The book concludes with an intervention by Jena McGill and Amy Salyzyn on how the increasing capabilities of big data methods and their "mainstreaming" might impact the Supreme Court of Canada. They argue that, in the not-too-distant future, judicial analytics can be expected to play a role in the appointments process, in cases as litigants seek to maximize their chances of success before the Court, and in evaluating the performance of judges. While some of these uses may increase transparency and accountability, there are reasons to be concerned about the access to justice implications of the privatization of judicial analytics. There is also the concern that the data generated by these methods may shed more heat than light, or may even be misleading, if they are not produced and interpreted in the right way. McGill and Salyzyn conclude that the use of judicial analytics must proceed with caution, informed by both its possible benefits and risks.

I.6 Conclusion

The process of developing this book has been a deeply iterative, team effort. It has required the research team to communicate across scholarly and disciplinary divides and go back and forth between data analysis and writing. While this process has been more challenging than anticipated, it has ultimately produced a more reflective research product. In particular, our law students, trained in programming and data analysis, played a vital role in extracting insights from the full text data.

As new methods emerge for examining institutions empirically, the toolkit for studying the Court will continue to expand. This is an exciting development for scholars of the Supreme Court, because it opens up new perspectives from which to study the Court, its processes, and its decisions.

1 A Bird's-Eye View of the Canadian Supreme Court

Wolfgang Alschner and
Keenan MacNeal

1.1 Introduction

Treating judicial opinions as data has a significant advantage: it adds a bird's-eye view to legal and institutional analysis. This book argues that legal analysis is at its best when it seeks to combine such a 30,000-foot-view with in-depth doctrinal analysis. In this chapter, we set the stage for such a mixed-methods approach. The chapter provides a high-level perspective on the data we gathered, the questions we tackled, and the broad patterns and trends we detected. This review provides readers with an overview of the lay of the land and establishes the foundation for subsequent chapters to zoom in and explore specific questions.

The chapter begins with a description of our dataset. Section 1.3 introduces the three lines of inquiry we pursue in this book and provides a preliminary analysis of those topics. Section 1.4 traces the evolution of the Court and highlights how data analysis reveals successive constitutional moments and landmark judgments. Section 1.5 looks at cleavages on the Court, tracking the evolution of dissent and showing how the growing voice of women transformed the bench. Section 1.6 turns to the Court's evolving judicial practice, with a particular emphasis on how treating text as data allows for rigorous analysis of writing style. With the stage set, the remainder of the book will explore the three themes in greater depth.

1.2 The Dataset

After receiving approval from the Supreme Court of Canada Registrar, we signed a research collaboration agreement with the Canadian Legal Information Institute (CanLII) to obtain the full text of the Court's decisions and its citations under a limited licence that included an obligation precluding the sharing of the full text data. In early 2020, we received data of 11,000 full text decisions and 1,100,000 individual citations to

DOI: 10.4324/9781003279112-2

and from those decisions.[1] We used both legal and data formatting considerations to determine the scope of our analysis. We could have started with the Court's inception in 1875, or in 1949, when the Supreme Court became the final court of appeal for Canada. However, we ultimately opted to focus on decisions from 1975 onwards, because it was in 1975 that the Court assumed control over its own docket. Moreover, decisions were formatted more consistently thereafter. Our "corpus" (the term is used to describe a collection of written material in quantitative text analysis) thus consisted of more than 4,100 Supreme Court decisions between January 1975 and December 2021.

While this core dataset was used for the bulk of our research, the pursuit of specific research questions made additional data collection and analysis necessary. For example, in the search for authoritative precedents, we exploited the entire network of cross-citations going back to the 1880s. Conversely, in relation to other research questions, for example, on the use of French versus English scholarship in private law cases, our analysis had to drill deeper than what our general dataset permitted and required additional data collection and analysis. Finally, Chapter 7, written by Veel and Glowach, uses a separate dataset assembled by the chapter authors on applications for leave to the Court.

We used a range of natural language processing techniques to extract metadata from our core dataset. Off-the-shelf data analysis packages were used to calculate simple statistics such as document length. However, tailored regular expressions, a set of programming rules that look for specific patterns in text, needed to be written to retrieve content elements that describe a decision in greater detail, from the area of law to the existence of dissent to the outcome. These extracted elements are summarized in Table 1.1. All content elements were checked manually for accuracy and were compared with existing databases containing similar information, where applicable. Apart from the full text, which we are not permitted to share based on our agreement with the Court and CanLII, we are making this data available in raw form for other researchers to use.[2] We are also

---

1 The initial plan was to mine all of those decisions in order to build a common dataset that would fuel the research behind the initial chapters of the book. However, two problems quickly became apparent. First, from a conceptual point of view, different legal research questions require different datasets. Second, formatting of the full text varied significantly, making it challenging to consistently extract insights from the entire dataset. As a result, we had to compromise on both fronts.

2 Alschner, Wolfgang; Mathen, Carissima; MacDonnell, Vanessa, 2023, "Supreme Court of Canada Dataset", https://doi.org/10.5683/SP3/3YFSXV, Borealis Dataverse.

Table 1.1 Information computationally extracted from SCC full texts

Content element	Description
Full text	Full text of the decision
Full text split by author(s)	Full text of majority, concurrent, or dissenting opinions with each author(s)
Main areas of law	Extracted main areas of law from decision headnotes with a further curated grouping into six areas of law
Length of decision	Length of full text in characters and words
Judges present	Names of judges who issued the decision
Chief justice	Name of chief justice of the court when decision was rendered
Origin of appeal	Province or territory from which the appeal originated
Delivery method	Whether decision was rendered in writing or orally
Appeal outcome	Whether appeal was dismissed or allowed

launching an accompanying webpage to filter this data and make it available in an interactive manner.[3]

The creation of this baseline dataset was extremely laborious. Varying formatting conventions, typos, interspersed non-English texts, and other anomalies made it challenging to craft logical information extraction rules that account for every eventuality. Further advances in machine learning, including the increased capabilities of large language models like GTP-4, are likely to assist in these tasks in future research projects and their conversational interphases may eventually allow for such analysis without the writing of computer code.

This metadata was the starting point for the analysis conducted for this book. Information about a decision's area of law, for example, could now be combined with citation data to zoom into constitutional precedents. Data on judges' gender could be used to quantify the number of words written by female justices. Beyond metadata analysis, we used other data science techniques to make sense of our corpus. We employed network analysis to create the web of precedents used by the Court. We also resorted to computational linguistic metrics, such as readability scores, to assess changes in language over time. Yet again, we have not exhausted the toolbox of potentially available computational techniques. In short, this chapter and this book generally provide illustrations of the ways in which the SCC corpus can be used but does not exhaust

---

3 https://www.uottawa.ca/faculty-law/common-law/research/legal-technology-lab/supreme-court

all its possibilities, leaving future researchers with opportunities to further exploit the data.

1.3 The Court's Evolution

The Supreme Court of Canada has evolved considerably over its nearly 150 years in existence. When the Court was established in 1875, Canada was part of the British Empire and the highest court of the land was the Judicial Committee of the Privy Council, located in London, England. The Supreme Court of Canada assumed final appellate jurisdiction in 1949, but only gained control over its docket in 1975 with the abolishment of most 'as-of-right' appeals. In short, the SCC was not born an apex court. It became one. Data science can help track that evolution. One way is to empirically map all citations that connect its decisions to identify the Court's most cited landmark cases.

Citation analysis provides a bird's-eye-view of how courts and their jurisprudence evolve.[4] Landmark rulings tend to be cited extensively in subsequent decisions – that's what makes them landmarks. In contrast, peripheral cases attract scant attention. Decisions that get cited a lot can tell us a great deal about the periods, judges, and conditions that produce influential rulings. Of particular interest are references by a court to its own prior case law. They create an (evolving) picture of how a court considers its own past. They come as close as it gets to a court's "autobiography".

These autobiographies naturally differ from court to court. In the context of United States Supreme Court, for example, researchers have found that decisions from the New Deal (1930/40s) and civil liberties eras (late 1960/1970) on average proved most influential in terms of attracting subsequent citations; by contrast, the 'activist' period under Chief Justice Warren, when the court overruled existing precedents in the 1950s and early 1960s, left less of a mark on subsequent cases producing few enduring landmark precedents.[5] A study of the International Court of Justice showed the opposite. The 1960s, when the World Court demonstrated growing assertiveness and activism to defend its independence after being challenged by newly decolonized states as pro-Western, coincided with

---

4 Iain Carmichael et al., "Examining the Evolution of Legal Precedent Through Citation Network Analysis" (2017) 96 NC L Rev 44; Urška Šadl & Henrik Palmer Olsen, "Can Quantitative Methods Complement Doctrinal Legal Studies? Using Citation Network and Corpus Linguistic Analysis to Understand International Courts" (2017) 30 Leiden J Intl L 327.
5 James H. Fowler & Sangick Jeon, "The Authority of Supreme Court Precedent" (2008) 30 Social Networks 16.

its most cited decisions.[6] In short, a court's self-citations tell the story of that court's unique history.

The Canadian Supreme Court is no exception. Its constitutional role evolved as Canada became progressively more independent from the United Kingdom and constitutional norms native to Canada developed. Using data on close to 40,000 intra-SCC citations between 1879 and 2020, Figure 1.1 tracks that evolving constitutional role by counting the average number of citations by later SCC rulings to the Court's earlier decisions. Most noticeable is the spike of highly cited cases in the mid-1980s, shortly after the passing of the *Constitution Act, 1982* and the associated *Charter of Rights and Freedoms*. No other period had had such lasting jurisprudential impact and so profoundly marked the Court's role. Eight out of ten of the most cited SCC decisions listed in Table 1.2 fall into that era. They deal with constitutional law questions, with *R v Oakes*, concerned with limitations on Charter rights, leading the way with 196 SCC cases citing it.

Yet, other periods also proved important. Take the 1880 *Parsons* decision, which concerned the division of power between the provinces and the federal government under the *Constitution Act, 1867*. Despite being more the 140 years old, *Parsons* remains one of the ten most cited SCC decisions and was most recently cited to in 2020. This speaks to the ongoing relevance of the Court's early case law, particularly as it relates to continuing debates on federalism. Similarly, the Court under Chief Justice Bora Laskin (1973–1984) rendered numerous highly cited decisions starting in the mid-1970s that revolved around the relationship between the federal government and the provinces.

The development of common law constitutional rights left their mark, too. The frequently cited *Alberta Press Act Reference*, decided in 1938, which found provincial laws interfering with freedom of expression *ultra vires* provincial powers, marked the beginning of the Court's 'implied bill of rights' jurisprudence. It was followed by a string of influential decisions drawing on civil liberties norms and values. Although it did not involve civil liberties *per se*, the era culminated with the 1959 decision of *Roncarelli v Duplessis*, a decision that invoked the unwritten principle of the rule of law to constrain the exercise of arbitrary executive power. Following the 1982 entrenchment of the Charter, the Court rendered many new and highly cited decisions which strengthened and gave shape to numerous civil liberties (referred to in Canada as rights and freedoms). They include the Court's third-most cited decision, *R v Big M Drug*

---

6 Wolfgang Alschner & Damien Charlotin, "The Growing Complexity of the International Court of Justice's Self-Citation Network" (2018) 29 European Journal of International Law 83.

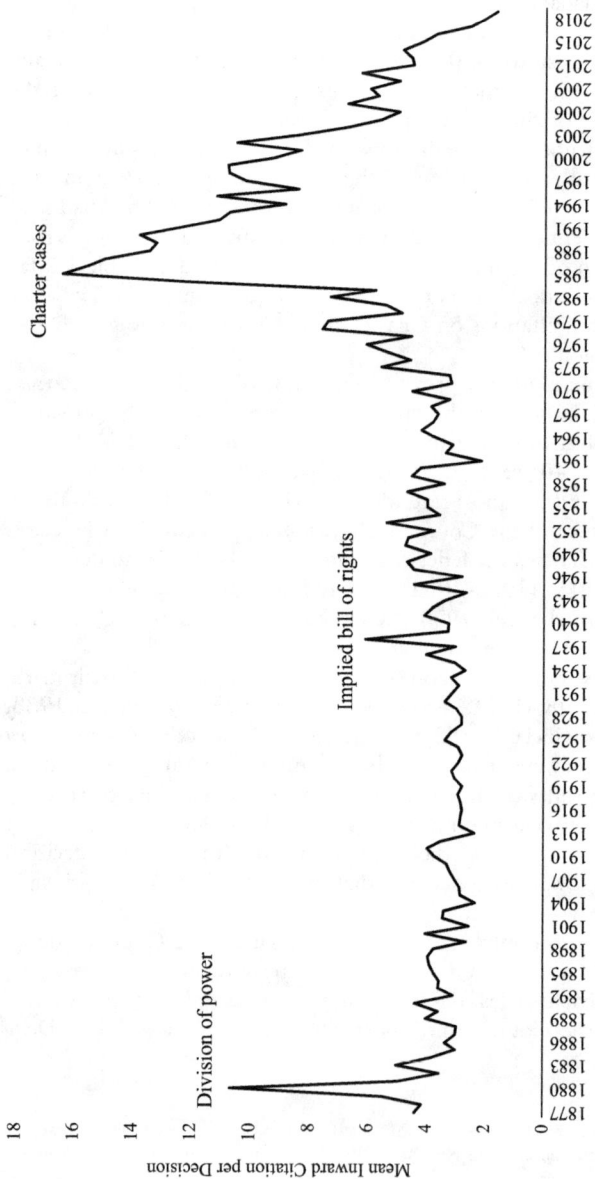

Figure 1.1 SCC's landmark judgments (average inward citation per decision)

Table 1.2 Most cited SCC decisions

Rank	Citation	Style of cause	Year	Indegree
1	1986 CanLII 46	*R v Oakes*	1986	**196**
2	1984 CanLII 33	*Hunter et al. v Southam Inc*	1984	175
3	1985 CanLII 69	*R v Big M Drug Mart Ltd*	1985	168
4	1998 CanLII 837	*Rizzo & Rizzo Shoes Ltd (Re)*	1998	**136**
5	1987 CanLII 84	*R v Collins*	1987	**128**
6	1985 CanLII 81	*Re BC Motor Vehicle Act*	1985	127
7	1989 CanLII 87	*Irwin Toy Ltd v Quebec (Attorney General)*	1989	109
8	1880 CanLII 6	*Citizens' and The Queen Insurance Cos v Parsons*	1880	**101**
9	1986 CanLII 12	*R v Edwards Books and Art Ltd*	1986	97
10	1987 CanLII 25	*R v Lyons*	1987	95

Mart, which invoked freedom of religion in striking down federal criminal legislation prohibiting commercial activity on Sundays.

Recent decisions have had less time to accumulate citations. Our data will record fewer citations to those decisions in the present, even if they turn out to be highly impactful in the future. Even by that standard, the drop in citations between the 1980s and early 2000s is remarkable, and is concordant with Peter McCormick's argument that adoption of the Charter created jurisprudential waves that have begun to flatten out.[7] That does not necessarily mean that the law is 'settled'. As MacDonnell & Macneal show in Chapter 2, which zooms in on the citations dealing with the concept of the separation of powers, constitutional controversies are very much alive. But, at least when measured using citations, the initial shock created by the Charter appears to have largely been absorbed.

Counting citations only scratches the surface. It is often more meaningful to think of citations as part of a citation *network*. The SCC's citation network is depicted in Figure 1.2 where each dot is a case and each line a citation between the cited and citing case. Some highly cited decisions may be important for niche areas of law but matter less for the overall development of jurisprudence. By situating case citations within the network of citations, peripheral cases can be distinguished from central ones. For example, *R v Oakes* and *R v Big M Drug Mart* are not only the most and third-most cited cases respectively, but they are also centrally located in the network of all citations. *Hunter v Southam*, the second

7 Peter J. McCormick, *The End of the Charter Revolution: Looking Back from the New Normal* (Toronto: University of Toronto Press Higher Education, 2014).

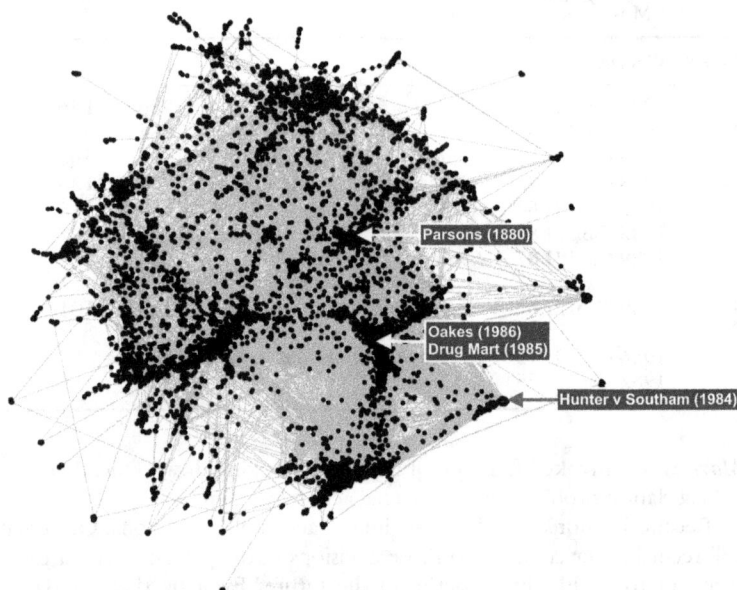

Figure 1.2 Citation network of the SCC

most cited case, in contrast, is more peripheral. Although *Parsons* is frequently cited, it is only cited by cases that relate to the division of power, while *Oakes* is referenced in almost every case dealing with Charter rights.

In addition, citation analysis can be combined with natural language processing to get at the question of *why* the Court has decided to cite to a given case in a particular context. Is the cite meant to distinguish the prior ruling from the case at issue, to overrule it, or to follow its reasoning? By mining the decisions for the context and content that surrounds citations, a more accurate picture forms about which citations matter and why. Chapter 3, by Alschner & St.-Hilaire, dives more deeply into network analysis and natural language processing and zooms into landmark cases to trace their rise and fall as precedents.

1.4 Cleavages on the Court

As the country's apex court, the Supreme Court of Canada is also a mirror of Canada's evolving society. Its decisions have played a crucial role in shaping Canada's legal system and, in turn, the nation's social landscape.

At the same time, the Supreme Court does not sit above and apart from the country's social fabric; as an institution and through its decisions, it is a reflection of the evolving views and values of Canadians. Divisions, disagreements, and differences that exist within society can therefore also manifest themselves as cleavages on the Court.

Perhaps nowhere is this clearer than in the Court's changing gender balance. On March 4, 1982, Justice Bertha Wilson became the first female justice ever to sit at the Supreme Court following her appointment by Prime Minister Pierre Trudeau. Before Justice Wilson's accession, 59 judges had been appointed to the bench over the Court's 107-year history. Every single one of them had been a man. Justice Wilson's appointment to the Court coincided – likely not coincidentally – with the enactment of the *Charter of Rights and Freedoms*, which protects against gender-based discrimination under Section 15 and Section 28.

The growing number and influence of women on the Supreme Court can be seen in our data, too. Our dataset begins in 1975, the year the Court celebrated its 100th birthday and, more importantly, gained control over its docket. Figure 1.3 shows the percentage of the Court's written output that was authored by women for each year in our dataset.[8] For the first seven years of our data, the Court's decisions were exclusively male-authored – as were the previous 100 years of decisions.[9]

Women have written a growing share of the Supreme Court's decisions since the appointment of Justice Wilson, although there has not yet been a year in which women authored more than 50% of the Court's output (nor have women ever composed a majority of the bench). This is likely to change soon. In 11 of the 16 years since 2005, women authored more than 40% of the Court's decisions, reaching a high of 49.6% in 2020.

We can also use our data to probe how the Court's male and female judges have differed in their approaches to the law. Before the year 2000, the women of the Court were notably less likely to join a majority judgment than were the men. In other words, the women wrote and/or joined dissenting and concurring judgments at a much higher rate (28%) than their male colleagues (18%). From 2000 onward, this gap almost disappears.

8 Output was measured on a per character basis, rather than on the basis of word count. Per curiam and other jointly written opinions were excluded prior to calculation (i.e. this analysis includes only opinions with a single author).

9 This may not be entirely true. According to records of Supreme Court clerks going back to 1967, the first female Supreme Court clerk was likely Susan M. Gibson, who clerked for Justice Hall in 1969. Clerks' uncredited writing is known to find its way into the Court's final decisions, and so it is possible, even likely, that Ms Gibson was the first woman to pen at least part of a Supreme Court decision.

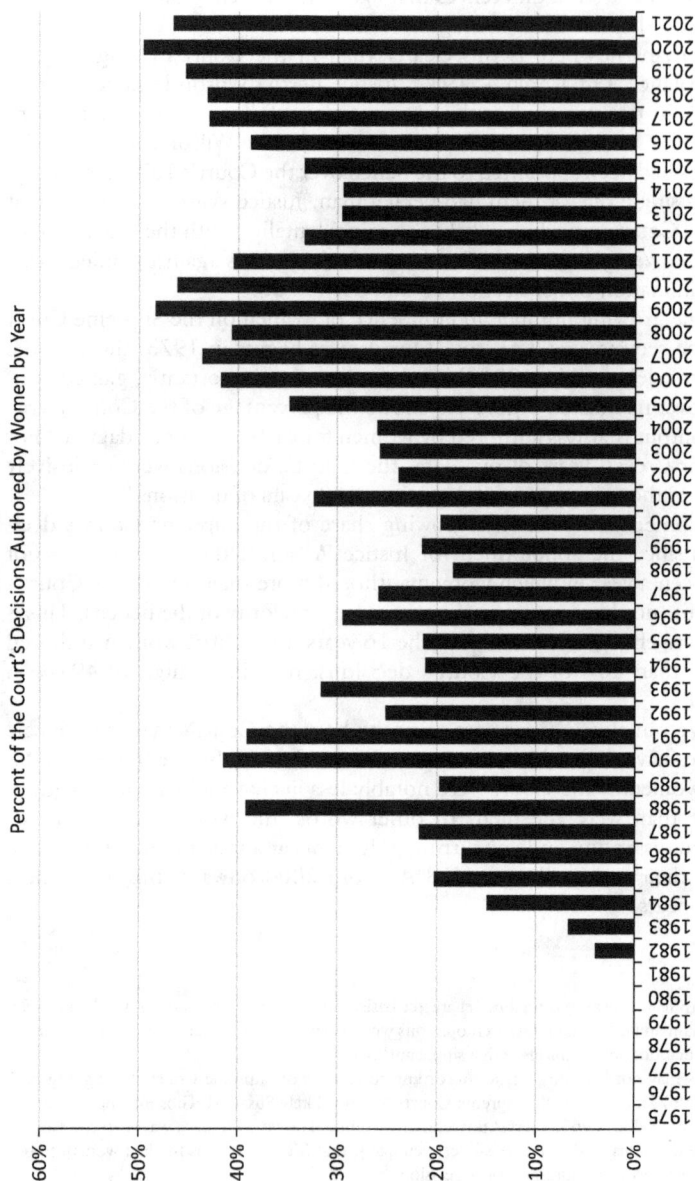

Figure 1.3 The growing voice of women on the bench

What explains this pattern? The first women on the Supreme Court inherited a legal tradition built almost exclusively by men. The systematic exclusion of women from the legal profession, especially at the highest levels, created blind spots in the Court's jurisprudence. The first female Supreme Court judges saw what their male colleagues and predecessors could not – or would not – see. Data helps turn the spotlight towards these blind spots.

By examining the linguistic content of the Court's decisions, we can detect patterns in how the Court deploys language and how the Court's writing has changed over time. A particularly stark example of the Court's changing use of language can be found in the Court's growing preference for "Ms." over "Mrs." as a feminine prefix, shown in Figure 1.4. "Miss" and "Mrs." are prefixes that indicate a woman's marital status, whereas the standard masculine prefix "Mr." does not indicate whether a man is married. Feminists have supported the use of the maritally neutral "Ms." since at least the 1940s.

Figure 1.4 shows how this broader socio-linguistic trend has appeared in the text of the Supreme Court of Canada's decisions. Each bar in the chart represents all uses of "Ms." or "Mrs." in a given year, with the ratio of black to white indicating the relative use of "Ms." versus "Mrs." The Court used the term "Ms." only a handful of times in the late 1970s and early 1980s. The frequency with which the Court used "Ms." jumped in 1986 and climbed throughout the 1990s, becoming the Court's clear preference by the mid-2000s. The last year in which the Court used "Mrs." more frequently than "Ms." was 2002. The scattered remaining uses of "Mrs." arise in cases where both spouses are implicated (e.g. "Mr. and Mrs. Suter's role…" in *R v Suter*).[10]

Text mining analysis can also be conducted in a more open-ended manner, rather than starting with pre-selected terms like "Ms." and "Mrs." One of our earliest and most surprising results was discovered using an open-ended text analysis technique for finding what data journalist Ben Blatt calls "cinnamon words" – rare words that a particular author uses at a much higher rate than is observed in a benchmark sample of other writers' work.[11] Cinnamon words can be thought of as an author's "trademark" language. Blatt applied the analysis to literary authors and found author–cinnamon word pairs like Jane Austen and "fancying" or Agatha Christie and "inquest".[12] We performed a cinnamon word analysis for

---

10 *R v Suter*, 2018 SCC 34 at para. 14.
11 Ben Blatt, *Nabokov's Favorite Word Is Mauve: What the Numbers Reveal about the Classis, Bestsellers, and Our Own Writing.* https://www.simonandschuster.com/books/Nabokovs-Favorite-Word-Is-Mauve/Ben-Blatt/9781501105401.
12 Ibid.

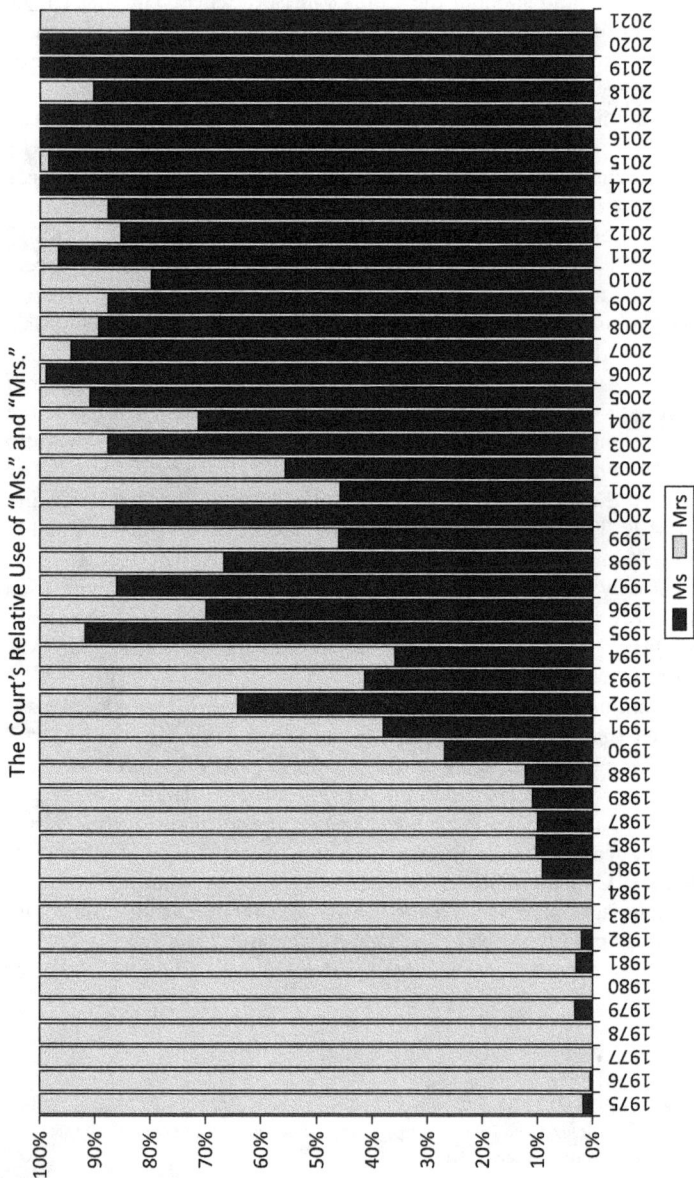

Figure 1.4 Changing patterns of curtesy

each judge on the Court during the era of Chief Justice Dickson, using as a benchmark the text of the 797 Supreme Court of Canada decisions from that period, as well as a random sample of 4,280 Supreme Court of the United States cases decided between 1950 and 2020.

One result stood out: Justice Wilson was the only judge who used the word "penis" across the more than 5,000 decisions that formed the benchmark for comparison. She used the word 13 times across five cases.[13] All five cases involved sexual assault, and four of them involved the sexual abuse of children. Justice Wilson used the word "penis" to accurately describe what happened during the assaults, in contrast to her colleague's use of more abstract language – Chief Justice Laskin spoke of "carnal" acts, while Justice Estey's preferred "indecency" – that tended to sanitize and obscure from the reader the violence that had been perpetrated.

The cleavage between male and female justices is, of course, not the only source of division at the Court. As a multilingual and multi-jurid-ical country, Canada's Supreme Court Justices come from French- and English-speaking jurisdictions and have variably been trained in common law and/or civil law. Skolnik and MacNeal's contribution to this collec-tion explores how these differences can produce cleavages at the Court.

In other ways, the Court has evolved countercyclically and provided stability in times of upheaval. Figure 1.5 traces the percentage of deci-sions with dissent across each of the last 45 years. In the late 1970s and early 1980s, tensions in Canadian society were at an all-time high. High inflation threatened livelihoods across the country and Quebec's inde-pendence movement put the future of the confederation in jeopardy. During this period of deep social division, the Court presented a remark-ably unified front, with one or more dissents registered in just one out of every ten cases.

The relative unanimity of the Court continued into the early Charter years, likely because the justices wished to speak with one voice as they established the foundations of a new era of Canadian constitutional law. The three most cited cases, *R v Oakes*, *Hunter et al v Southam Inc*, and *R v Big M Drug Mart Ltd*, all likely owe their preeminence to that addi-tional legitimacy.

Disagreement has since picked up. The share of cases per year with dis-sents rose in the late 1980s to between 20% and 30%. This range remained relatively stable from 1990 to 2015, with a few exceptions. In the last six years of our data, dissent rates have climbed rapidly, reaching an all-time high in 2018 when almost half of all decisions included a dissent. Chapter 4, by Mathen et al., looks at these trends in more depth.

---

13 *R v Robertson*, [1987] 1 SCR 918; *R v Paré*, [1987] 2 SCR 618; *R v Provo*, [1989] 2 SCR 3; *R v B (G)*, [1990] 2 SCR 3; *R v B (G)*, [1990] 2 SCR 57.

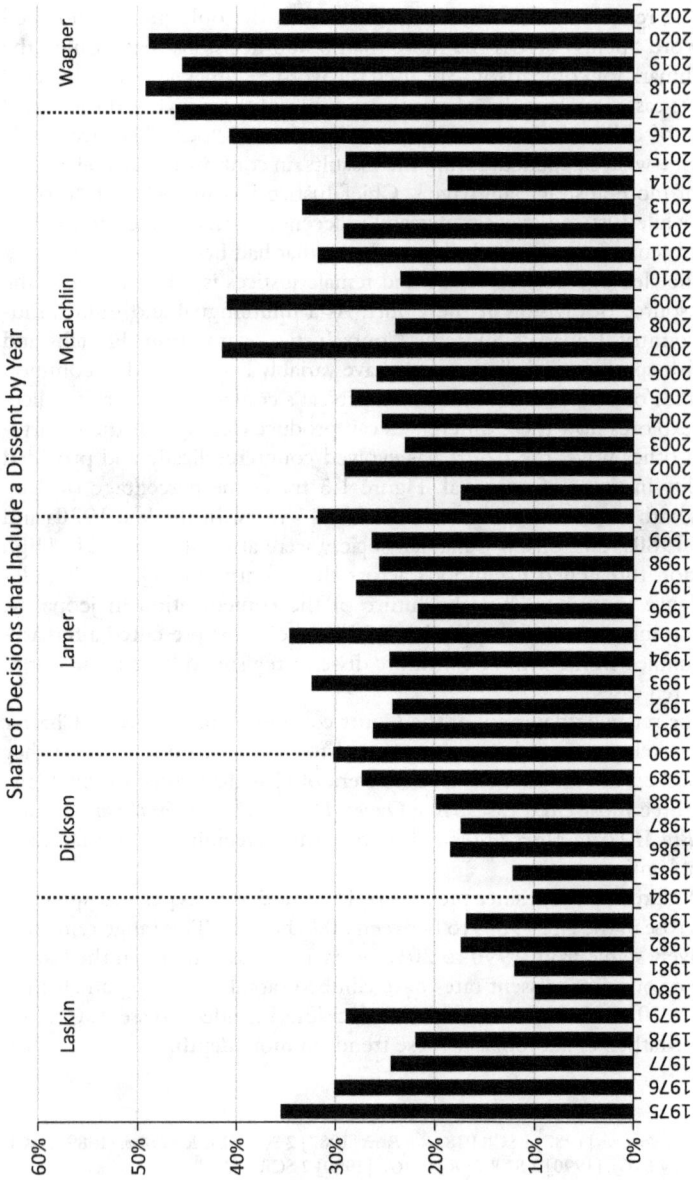

Figure 1.5 The ebb and flow of dissents

1.5 Judicial Practice

Beyond exploring the Court's evolution and its divisions, the bird's-eye perspective provided by data science techniques enables researchers to study the Supreme Court of Canada from a very practical perspective. Justices have to make choices. First, they have to select which and how many cases are granted leave to appeal. Second, they have to come to a decision on the cases they selected. Third, they have to communicate their decision – typically in writing. Our dataset sheds light on all three of these stages.

Our dataset suggests that justices have used the control over their docket to manage the number of cases heard each year. Figure 1.6 shows that in the pre-Charter years, the Court heard more than 100 cases per year on average. After the introduction of the Charter in 1982, the Court's yearly caseload dropped below 100 cases for five years, before returning to its prior cadence. The Court continued to hear more than 100 cases per year until the second half of the 1990s, when the number of cases heard each year dropped to a rate of about 60 per year, which has remained more or less constant since then. While our data can shed light on the cases heard, it is blind to the many potential cases that the Court rejected. To fill this crucial knowledge gap, Chapter 6 introduces a project to collect data on Leaves to Appeal both to predict the odds of a case making it to the Court and to systematically describe the types of appeals that end up before the Court.

As for the cases that make it to the Court, our data suggests that although the number of cases heard by the Court has fallen, the length of the Court's decisions has increased significantly. In the 1970s, the Court's majority opinions averaged about 3,500 words in length. The average length of majority opinions increased to almost 5,000 words in the years following the Charter's enactment in 1982, paralleling the decline in cases heard during that period. As the number of cases before the Court fell again in the late 1990s, the average length of majority opinions increased to more than 8,000 words, reaching a high of almost 9,500 words in 2021. In short, as the number of cases heard by the Court has fallen by almost half, the average length of majority opinions has increased by a factor of almost three. While the reasons behind this change are likely complex, complexity may be a reason in itself. The average Supreme Court decision in 1975 cited four prior cases. This number has since risen to more than 20 decisions by 2020. Judges have to digest more case law and more precedents than ever.

Turning to the second set of choices, the justices must decide whether or not to allow an appeal. Using natural language processing, we have investigated the last paragraphs of every decision in order to assess whether an appeal was allowed or dismissed. We carefully fine-tuned and validated our approach through the manual review of a large sample of

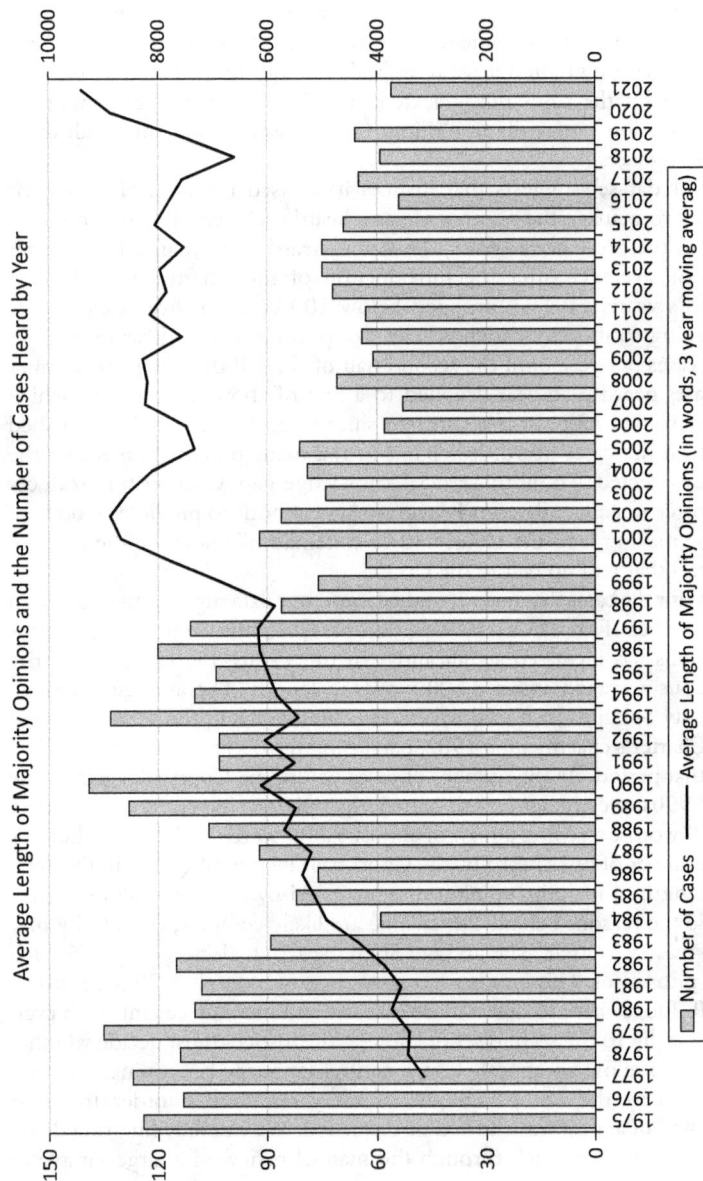

Average Length of Majority Opinions and the Number of Cases Heard by Year

Number of Cases — Average Length of Majority Opinions (in words, 3 year moving averag)

Figure 1.6 Fewer, but longer decisions

decisions. The resulting data allows us to group decisions by outcomes. Surprisingly, as we show in Figure 1.7, success rates differ markedly by the geographic origin of the case. Although the Supreme Court hears more appeals from Ontario than from any other province, appellants tend to succeed only in one out of three cases from Ontario compared to every second case from the Maritimes.

Outcome variables are also crucial for training predictive algorithms and for drawing causal inferences regarding the factors that make a case succeed. While our data mining efforts have not been extensive enough to warrant either prediction or causal inferences, we see great research and practicable opportunities in both of these areas. Jena McGill and Amy Salyzyn's contribution thinks ahead to a time when metrics, including on Supreme Court Justices, are more abundant and considers the resulting practical, ethical, and normative implications.

Our existing corpus can, however, provide insights into the last phase of judicial practice – how judges communicate their decisions. There are several reasons why we should care how judges write their decisions. First, writing style can provide clues about authorship. Bodwin et al., for example, tracked variation in writing styles using function words (e.g. "this", "then", "there") in Supreme Court decisions to assess whether law clerks

Portion of Appeals Allowed by Jurisdiction of Origin
(Prairies = AB, SK, MB; Maritimes = NB, NS, NFLD, PEI)

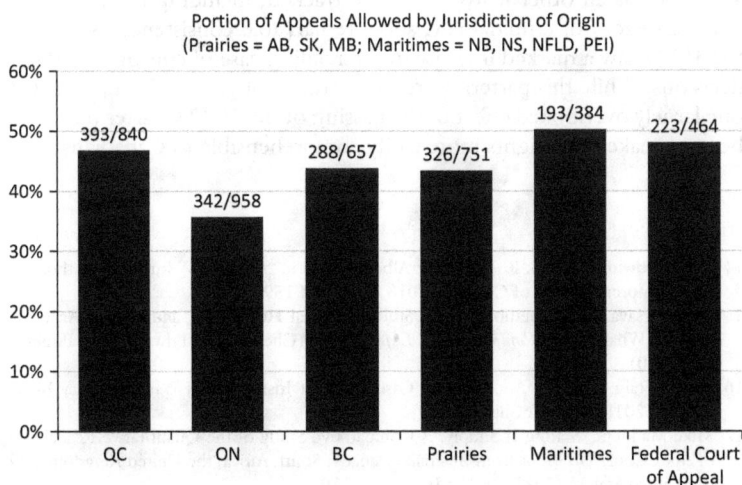

Figure 1.7 Most appeals come from Ontario, but their success rates are the lowest

increasingly write judicial opinions.[14] Second, writing style allows judges to stand out.[15] For example, Elaine Craig has studied the "literary judgments" penned by David Watts of the Ontario Court of Appeal that garnered him public and media attention.[16] Third, on an institutional level, writing style matters in terms of how courts communicate their decisions. For example, systematically low readability levels in judicial writings have been flagged as an access to justice barrier (e.g. due to legalese or complex sentence structure).[17]

Our data brings differences in writing style into sharp focus. Consider readability. The most common readability measure is Flesch reading ease. Although it is simple – the formula is based on average sentence length and word and syllable counts – it has been shown to effectively track reading ease and is widely used. By that measure, SCC decisions between 1975 and 2021 average a Flesch Reading Ease Score of around 47, meaning they require college-level education to be understood. That score has remained stable over time and varies little between dissenting and majority opinions.

There is, however, important variation between judges and across areas of law. Chief Judge Dickson, who has been known to possess "a clear and direct writing style",[18] scores higher on the reading ease ladder and can make himself understood to high-school graduates. In contrast, most of Judge Ritchie's solely authored decisions require reading abilities of university graduate students and contain sentences that are on average 50% longer than Dickson's. In terms of areas of law, reading ease has improved significantly in constitutional law. As can be seen in Figure 1.8, whereas all other fields of law we tracked, including the most pervasive category of criminal law, show remarkable consistency over time, the 1980s saw a marked increase in the reading ease of constitutional law decisions. While this pattern warrants further study, it could suggest that one largely overlooked effect of the passing of the 1982 Charter may have been to make basic rights more easily comprehensible to Canadians.

---

14 Kelly Bodwin, Jeffrey S. Rosenthal, & Albert H. Yoon, "Opinion Writing and Authorship on the Supreme Court of Canada" (2013) 63 UTLJ 159.

15 Nina Varsava, "Computational Legal Studies, Digital Humanities, and Textual Analysis" in Ryan Whalen, ed., *Computational Legal Studies* (Cheltenham: Edward Elgar Publishing, 2020).

16 Elaine Craig, "Judicial Audiences: A Case Study of Justice David Watt's Literary Judgments" (2018) 64:2 McGill LJ 369.

17 Mike Madden, "Stating It Simply: A Comparative Study of the Quantitative Readability of Apex Court Decisions from Australia, Canada, South Africa, the United Kingdom, and the United States" (2021) 23 NC JL & Tech 270.

18 Robert J. Sharpe, Kent Roach, & Osgoode Society for Canadian Legal History, *Brian Dickson: A Judge's Journey* (Toronto: University of Toronto Press, 2003) at 5.

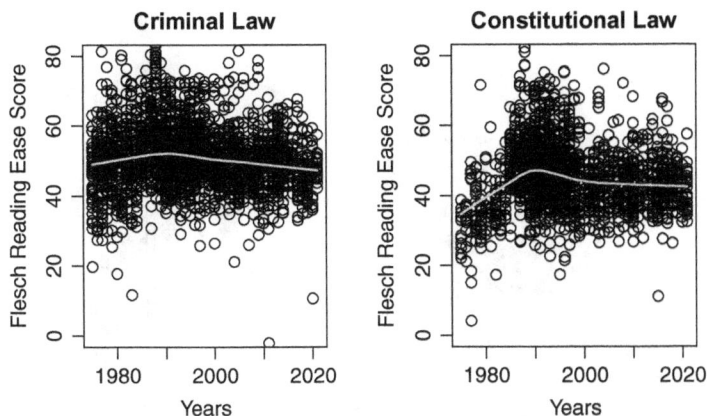

Figure 1.8 Constitutional decisions have become more readable, criminal law ones not

Finally, sentiment analysis can shed light on another aspect of writing style – the emotive tone of text. The simplest and most common way to conduct such analysis is by counting specific words associated with different sentiments, for example, positive and negative emotions. Collections of these sentiment-word pairings are called lexicons or sentiment dictionaries. Whether sentiment dictionaries can be meaningfully applied to the law therefore depends on the research question and dictionary.[19] It is important to remember that judicial decisions are written differently to social media posts or financial statements; judges rarely cast their opinions in exuberant or gloomy language, and words that may have a positive or negative connotation in natural language may have different and at times opposite connotations in law.[20]

The conceptual case for the use of sentiment analysis is strongest for uncertainty dictionaries. These dictionaries collect words that signal ambiguity, like "could", "doubt", or "somewhat". In law, there are at least two research questions for which tracking ambiguity may be useful. First, apex courts routinely resolve judicial disagreements that caused

19 For a successful application in the legal context, see Marc L. Busch & Krzysztof J. Pelc, "Words Matter: How WTO Rulings Handle Controversy" (2019) International Studies Quarterly, https://academic.oup.com/isq/advance-article/doi/10.1093/isq/sqz025 /5499120 (accessed July 19, 2019).
20 For example, a decision that "awards damages", although coded as negative in a sentiment dictionary, is good news for claimants.

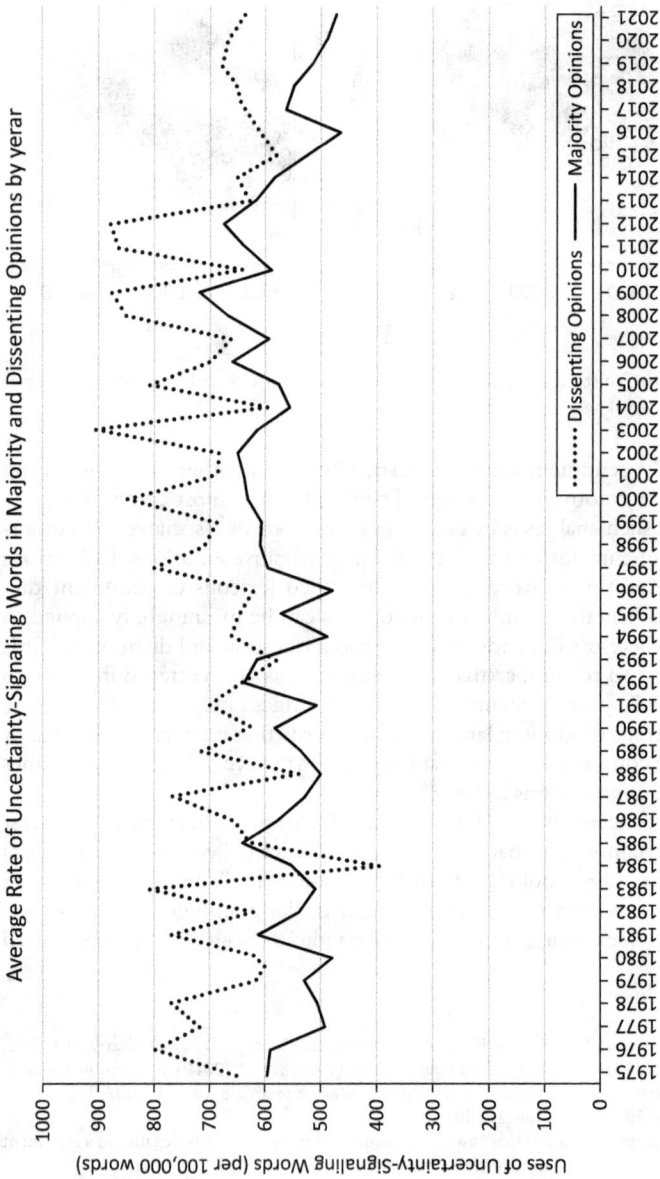

Figure 1.9 Dissenting opinions often cast doubt

uncertainty in the past. Once judicial questions go from being "unsettled" to "settled", one should observe a decline in uncertainty-signalling language. Second, one of the functions of dissent is to challenge the reasoning of the majority, to cast doubt on the strengths of their arguments, and to advocate for change. One can thus expect dissents to include more uncertainty-related words. Applying the Loughran-McDonald uncertainty dictionary to our corpus, we find corroborating evidence for both assumptions. When limited to constitutional law, uncertainty words declined in the early 1980s with the passing of the Charter, mirroring the readability trend discussed above, suggesting that controversial questions of law became more settled. As can be seen in Figure 1.9, we also find that dissents contain around 20% more uncertainty words than majority opinions. Sentiment analysis of full text thus has a role to play – but needs to be used in the right context to obtain meaningful results.

1.6 Conclusion

This chapter introduced the dataset and showcased how data analysis can assist in studying legal and socio-legal questions relating to the Supreme Court at scale. The bird's-eye view shed light on the Court's evolution, its cleavages, and its judicial practice. With this background in mind, the remainder of this book will zoom into each of these issues. Moreover, we hope that the illustrations introduced in the chapters have whetted the appetite of future researchers to use our dataset to explore questions and applications not contemplated in this book.

Part 1
Evolution of the Court

2 Four Stories about Canada's Separation of Powers Doctrine

Vanessa MacDonnell and
Keenan MacNeal[1]

2.1 Introduction

In Canada, as in other Westminster states, there are good reasons to question the salience of the separation of powers as a constitutional principle.[2] After all, there is no "strict" separation of powers between the executive, legislative, and judicial branches; in at least some contexts, the overlap is significant.[3] Until recently, moreover, the concept has attracted relatively little attention from the Supreme Court of Canada. The first reference to the separation of powers appeared just prior to the enactment of the *Canadian Charter of Rights and Freedoms,* and for the first decade of the principle's formal judicial existence, the case law was characterized by

1 Vanessa MacDonnell is an Associate Professor at the University of Ottawa Faculty of Law and Co-Director of the uOttawa Public Centre. Keenan Macneal graduated with a juris doctor (JD) from the University of Ottawa Faculty of Law in 2023. We are grateful to Leo Russomanno, Eric Adams, Michael Pal, Jeremy Opolsky, Paul-Erik Veel, Amy Salyzyn, Jena McGill, Samuel Singer, Carissima Mathen, Wolfgang Alschner, Terry Skolnik, Stephen Bindman, Jacqueline Burkell, Jonathan Khan, and participants in conferences at UBC and the Université Jean Monnet for comments and suggestions. We thank Kelley Humber for research assistance. This chapter is current to December 31, 2022, with the exception of the keyness analysis described in Part 2.3.3, which includes cases to the end of 2021 only.
2 Aileen Kavanagh, "The Constitutional Separation of Powers" in David Dyzenhaus and Malcolm Thorburn, eds, *Philosophical Foundations of Constitutional Law* (Oxford: Oxford University Press, 2016) 221; Roger Masterman and Se-shauna Wheatle, "Unpacking Separation of Powers : Judicial Independence, Sovereignty and Conceptual Flexibility in the UK Constitution" 2017 Public Law 469; David Schneiderman, "The Separation of Powers and Constitutional Balance at the McLachlin Court" in Marcus Moore and Daniel Jutras, eds, *Canada's Chief Justice: Beverley McLachlin's Legacy of Law and Leadership* (Toronto: LexisNexis Canada, 2018) 137. The meaning of the separation of powers is contested, as this chapter demonstrates. However, it can be understood at a very high level as the division of state functions between the executive, legislative, and judicial branches. See generally Yan Campagnolo, *Behind Closed Doors: The Law and Politics of Cabinet Secrecy* (Vancouver: UBC Press, 2021) at 203.
3 *Reference re Secession of Quebec,* [1998] 2 SCR 217 at paras 13, 15.

DOI: 10.4324/9781003279112-4

active disagreement about whether it was part of Canadian constitutional law at all.[4]

In recent years, however, there has been a noticeable uptick in references to the separation of powers in the Supreme Court's jurisprudence. The very spare descriptions of the concept that dominated the early case law have given way to more fulsome discussions of the principle.[5] This raises the question of what is driving increased resort to the principle, and what value(s) the Supreme Court is upholding when it invokes the separation of powers in its jurisprudence.[6]

In this chapter, we employ systematic doctrinal analysis to examine Canada's separation of powers doctrine.[7] We adopt this approach for two reasons. First, systematic analysis allows us to track references to the separation of powers by the Supreme Court over time, unencumbered by prior assumptions about the principle and its role in the jurisprudence. This approach is particularly useful in a context in which, as here, there is active disagreement in the scholarship about the nature and importance of the principle. In addition, examining references to the principle alongside other, related principles, such as parliamentary sovereignty, judicial independence, and prosecutorial independence may help identify the interests that are being secured when the Court invokes the separation of powers.[8] Because the form of systematic analysis we adopt may not fully capture how the principle has developed over time, we also engage in a close reading of all Supreme Court cases in which the term has appeared. This allows us to further identify trends in the case law, and to elucidate the meaning of the separation of powers as a constitutional principle.

Four stories emerge from our analysis. The first is that references to the separation of powers seem to be on the rise. Those who question its significance in Canada might be surprised to learn that the Supreme Court has referred to the principle in 48 cases since 1975, and in 21 cases

---

4 Carissima Mathen, *Courts without Cases: The Law and Politics of Advisory Opinions* (Oxford: Hart Publishing, 2019).
5 Mary Liston, "Bringing the Mixed Constitution Back In" (2021) 30:4 Constitutional Forum 9 at 11.
6 Jeremy Waldron, "Separation of Powers in Thought and Practice" (2013) 54 Boston College L Rev 433; Schneiderman, *supra* note 1; Warren Newman, "The Rule of Law, the Separation of Powers and Judicial Independence in Canada" in Peter Oliver, Patrick Macklem, and Nathalie Des Rosiers, eds, *The Oxford Handbook of the Canadian Constitution* (Oxford: Oxford University Press, 2017) 1031 at 1040; Kavanagh, *supra* note 1 at 221–223.
7 See William Baude, Adam Chilton, and Anup Malani, "Making Doctrinal Work More Rigorous: Lessons from Systematic Reviews" (2017) 84 U Chicago L Rev 37.
8 In conducting this systematic analysis, we relied on a mix of legal data analytics and hand coding of variables.

in the last decade.[9] In 2021, the separation of powers was mentioned in 20% of all cases in which the Court issued a written opinion. In short, it would appear that the principle is being invoked with greater frequency, and discussed in greater detail, than ever before.

The second story is that this trend is being led by specific judges. Justice Karakatsanis has discussed the principle in more cases than any other justice, though Justices Brown, Rowe, and Côté have also invoked the principle with some frequency in recent years. Justice Karakatsanis is also the justice on the current court who has authored the most majority judgments referring to the separation of powers.

The third story is that, contrary to what might be assumed, the principle has been invoked to protect the sphere of action of the legislature, the executive, and the courts. Judges of the Court not only invoke the separation of powers when they think that an issue falls outside of their purview; they also refer to the principle when they conclude that the judiciary has particular expertise in a matter, such as where the rule of law and/or judicial independence is concerned. In other words, when the Court invokes the separation of powers, it is not invariably to decline to intervene in a matter in deference to the political branches.

The final story is that the justices of the Supreme Court appear to be largely in agreement as regards the meaning of the separation of powers as a concept. The Court's view is summarized well by Warren Newman, who writes that the separation of powers means that each branch has particular competencies that must be respected if a "constitutional equilibrium" is to be maintained between the organs of state.[10] However, members of the Court are far less likely to agree with each other on how the principle applies in practice. This has resulted in several cases in which the separation of powers forms the basis of a dissent.

We begin this chapter with a brief review of the scholarship on the separation of powers. In Section 2.3, we elaborate on the four stories introduced above, before concluding in Section 2.4.

2.2 Scholarship on the Separation of Powers

Jacob Levy has argued that "The separation of powers might well be *the* crucial concept in what we have come to think of as constitutionalism or constitutional government".[11] And yet, as Aileen Kavanagh notes, "In

---

9 The case set from which this study draws contains 4,198 cases, of which 894 are constitutional cases.

10 Newman, *supra* note 5 at 1043.

11 Jacob T. Levy, "The Separation of Powers and the Challenge to Constitutional Democracy" (2020) 25:1 Rev Const Stud 1.

the panoply of principles regulating constitutional government, the separation of powers occupies a position of deep ambivalence".[12] Kavanagh offers several reasons for this ambivalence. One is the disconnect between the idea of separation and the reality of functional overlap between the branches of state in a parliamentary democracy. Other reasons include a lack of clarity regarding the relationship between the separation of powers and the idea of checks and balances (which, as Kavanagh notes, seems to imply some degree of institutional overlap), the absence of the administrative state from contemporary descriptions of the separation of powers, and disagreement over the purposes the separation of powers is thought to fulfil.[13]

Canadian scholars have taken a range of positions on the separation of powers and its role in Canadian constitutional law. Peter Hogg was notably dismissive of the principle, stating that "There is no general 'separation of powers' in the *Constitution Act, 1867*. The Act does not separate the legislative, executive and judicial functions and insist that each branch of government exercise only 'its own' functions".[14] He also doubted the concept's utility in a system of responsible government, noting that, in reality, cabinet largely dictates the activities of Parliament.[15]

Others have written more favourably about the status of the separation of powers, though they have also noted that case law on the principle remains in its infancy.[16] Writing in 2021, Mary Liston concluded that "the separation of powers is a fundamental architectural principle in Canadian public law jurisprudence", but that "we do not yet have a general separation of powers doctrine".[17] For the moment, she said, the case law "remains rather sleek, if not skeletal, in content".[18] In 2017, Warren Newman referred to the separation of powers as a "still emerging principle".[19] He nevertheless suggested that a rationale for the prin-

---

12 Kavanagh, *supra* note 1 at 221. See also Masterman and Wheatle, *supra* note 1; Han-Ru Zhou, François Chevrette, and Herbert Marx, *Constitutional Law: Fundamental Principles* (Montréal: Les Editions Thémis, 2020) at 381; Schneiderman, *supra* note 1.

13 Kavanagh, *supra* note 1 at 221–223.

14 Peter W. Hogg, *Constitutional Law in Canada, Loose-Leaf* (Toronto: Carswell, 1995) at 7.15. Dennis Baker argues that Hogg's position reflects the "orthodoxy" when it comes to the separation of powers. See Dennis Baker, *Not Quite Supreme: The Courts and Coordinate Constitutional Interpretation* (Montreal & Kingston: McGill-Queen's University Press, 2010) at 9–10. See also James B. Kelly, *Governing with the Charter: Legislative and Judicial Activism and Framers' Intent* (Vancouver: UBC Press, 2005) at 81.

15 Hogg, *supra* note 13 at 9.12. See also Zhou, Chevrette, and Marx, *supra* note 11 at 382; Campagnolo, *supra* note 1 at 203.

16 See, for example, Newman, *supra* note 5 at 1039, 1041.

17 Liston, *supra* note 4 at 9, 17.

18 Ibid. at 11.

19 Newman, *supra* note 5 at 1039.

ciple could be discerned in the case law. The separation of powers, he explained, reflects "deep concern with the necessity of maintaining a delicate balance in a constitutional democracy: of sustaining an appropriate constitutional equilibrium amongst the executive, legislative, and judicial branches, so that no branch may plausibly sustain a claim of absolute power, to the detriment of the other branches".[20]

Other scholars have tended to focus on the implications of separating state powers. Carissima Mathen has argued that the central tenet of Canada's separation of powers doctrine is that "each branch should stay in its respective 'lane'".[21] In a 2018 review of the McLachlin Court's separation of powers cases, David Schneiderman concluded that the principle emphasizes a "sort of sympathetic respect".[22] However, he also argued that the Supreme Court has deployed the separation of powers strategically, particularly where judicial interests are at play.[23] And Dennis Baker's work on coordinate construction argues for a "partial agency" view of the separation of powers, under which a "degree of mixing of functional powers across branches" is permitted and even encouraged.[24]

2.3 Four Stories about Canada's Separation of Powers Doctrine

As this brief review makes clear, there remains a great deal of uncertainty about the nature and role of the separation of powers in Canadian constitutional law. In this section, we attempt to provide some clarity regarding the current state of the doctrine through a systematic doctrinal analysis of the case law. Our conclusions in this section are also supported by a close reading of each Supreme Court case in which the term "separation of powers" has appeared.

It is important to acknowledge both the strengths and weaknesses of this approach. One benefit of adopting a systematic approach is that it has the potential to reveal patterns in the jurisprudence that might otherwise go unrecognized.[25] The current academic discourse on the separation of powers is notable for its active disagreement over what role, if any, the principle plays in contemporary constitutional law. This is at least partly an empirical question. Tracking references to the separation of powers in

20 Ibid. at 1043.
21 Mathen, *supra* note 3 at 2020.
22 Schneiderman, *supra* note 1.
23 Ibid.
24 Baker, *supra* note 13 at 11.
25 We are grateful to Wolfgang Alschner for this insight.

the jurisprudence is therefore a useful way of investigating the nature and salience of the separation of powers in Canadian constitutional law.

The major shortcoming of this approach is that it only examines how the separation of powers has been treated by the Supreme Court of Canada; it does not examine how the principle is understood by the other branches of state. Moreover, the method we adopt focuses on the insights that can be gained by tracking the term "separation of power" systematically in the jurisprudence, supported by a close reading of the case law. It does not attempt to provide a comprehensive picture of how the Court understands the separation of powers. Indeed, one of the most important separation of powers cases to be decided by the Supreme Court of Canada, the *New Brunswick Broadcasting Case*, does not use the term "separation of powers" and, as such, does not fall within our case set.[26] Closely tracking and reflecting on the use of the separation of powers principle nonetheless reveals important findings, especially when these findings are considered as data points in a larger discussion.[27]

2.3.1 References to the Separation of Powers Appear to Be Increasing

We begin with the first story, which is that references to the separation of powers appear to be increasing. (Figure 2.1)

Since 1975, the Supreme Court has referred to the term "separation of power" in 48 cases. As might be expected, the concept is discussed most frequently in constitutional cases. 77% of the cases containing the term were constitutional cases (37 of 48), while the remaining 23% (11 of 48) were non-constitutional. For reference, constitutional cases make up 21% of all Supreme Court cases since 1975.

The Court's decision was unanimous in one third of the cases (16 of 48 or 33%), a far lower rate of unanimity than observed across all cases (2,538 of 4,198, or slightly above 60%). Of the remaining 32 non-unanimous decisions, 17 include a concurrence and 21 include a dissent (six include both a concurrence and dissent). Although "separation of power"

---

26 *New Brunswick Broadcasting Co v Nova Scotia (Speaker of the House of Assembly)*, [1993] 1 SCR 319.

27 Another possible limitation is that some types of separation of powers issues are more likely to reach the courts than others. For instance, the Court is unlikely to be called upon to decide a separation of powers issue involving the executive and the legislature with any frequency, though there are of course examples of such cases: see, for example, *Mikisew Cree First Nation v Canada (Governor General in Council)*, 2018 SCC 40; *References re Greenhouse Gas Pollution Pricing Act*, 2021 SCC 11. It is more likely to apply the separation of powers in matters involving the judiciary and one of the other two branches of state.

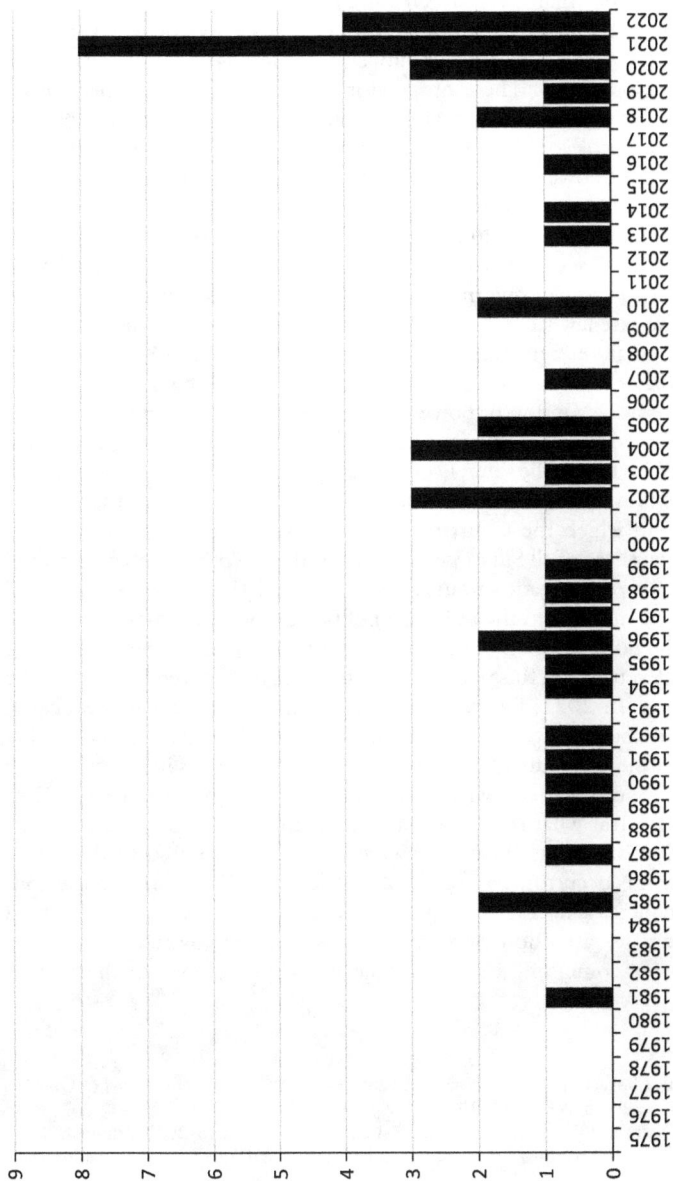

Figure 2.1 Cases referencing "Separation of Power" by year

is more likely to appear in cases that divided the Court, the term was used in more than one opinion in only seven cases (see Appendix A).

Usage of the term "separation of powers" can also be examined by opinion, rather than by case. Of the 58 separate opinions in which the separation of powers is mentioned, 60% were majority opinions (35 opinions), 19% were concurring opinions (11 opinions), and 20% were dissents (12 opinions). These proportions are each within one percentage point of the proportions of majority, concurring, and dissenting opinions across the whole dataset. Taken together, these factors suggest that the separation of powers is not a concept that is confined to concurring and dissenting judgments. (Figure 2.2)

Between 2018 and 2022, the Court used the term "separation of power" 108 times in 26 separate opinions across 18 cases. These 18 cases represent more than one third of all references to the separation of powers in the case law since 1975 (18/48 or 38%). The 26 opinions account for 44% of all references in the Court's opinions since 1982 (108/246). Since 2018, in other words, both the frequency and the density of references to the separation of powers appear to have been increasing.

The importance of this apparent increase becomes more evident when we consider that while references to the separation of powers were increasing, the number of cases the Court heard was falling, as was the number of cases in which the Court provided full written reasons.[28] Figure 2.3 shows the share of all Supreme Court cases that involved the separation of powers for each decade of our dataset.[29] Since 2015, more than 4% of all cases have mentioned the separation of powers, which is more than three times the portion (1.25%) that such cases represented in the 1995–2004 period. Even within this particularly active period, the trend appears to be increasing. In 2021, for example, the Supreme Court decided 56 cases. It provided full written reasons in only 36 of those cases. This means that in 2021, the Court mentioned the separation of powers in one fifth of all cases in which it issued a written decision (8 out of 36 cases). (Figure 2.4)

It is unclear what is driving this apparent increase in references to the separation of powers. Further research would be required to determine whether it is occurring as a result of increased judicial interest in the concept, an increase in cases raising separation of powers issues being granted leave, greater attention by parties, interveners, or lower courts to the concept, or something else.[30] Without knowing more about the reasons

---

28 See Alex Bogach, Jeremy Opolsky, and Paul-Erik Veel, "The Supreme Court of Canada's From the Bench Decisions" (2022) 74 SCLR (2d) 251.

29 Note that the 2015–2022 period only includes seven years (2015–2022 inclusive).

30 We are grateful to Jonathan Khan, Carissima Mathen, and Amy Salyzyn for raising some of these possibilities.

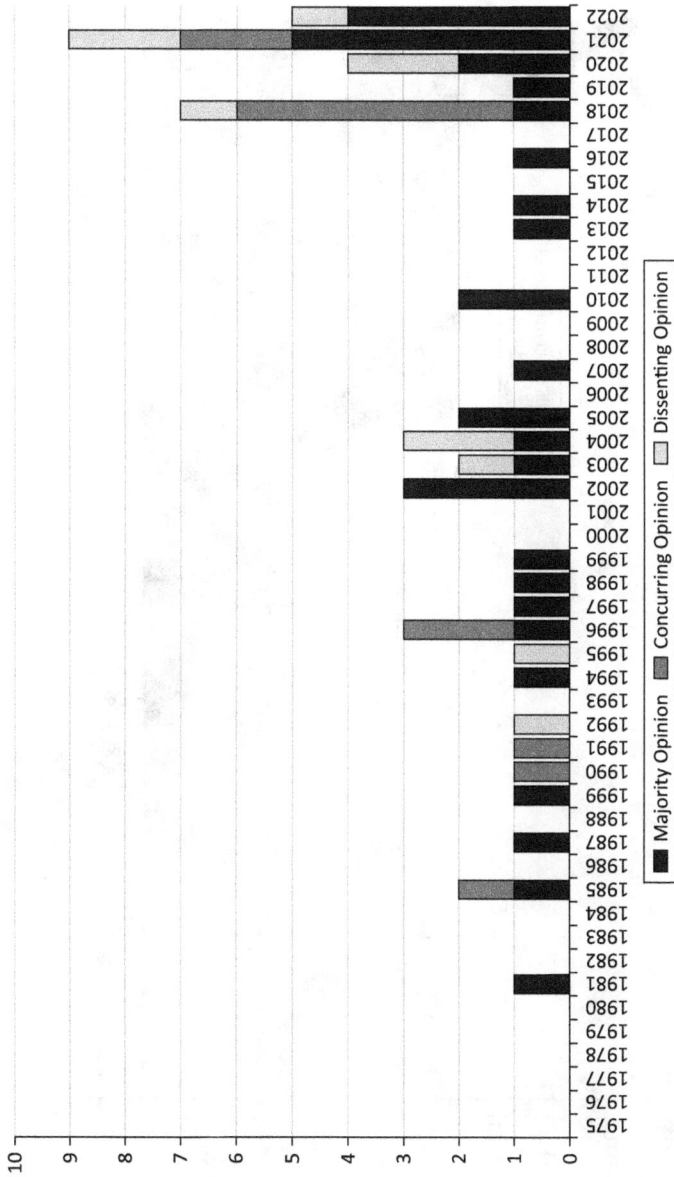

Figure 2.2 Opinions discussing "Separation of Power" by year and opinion type

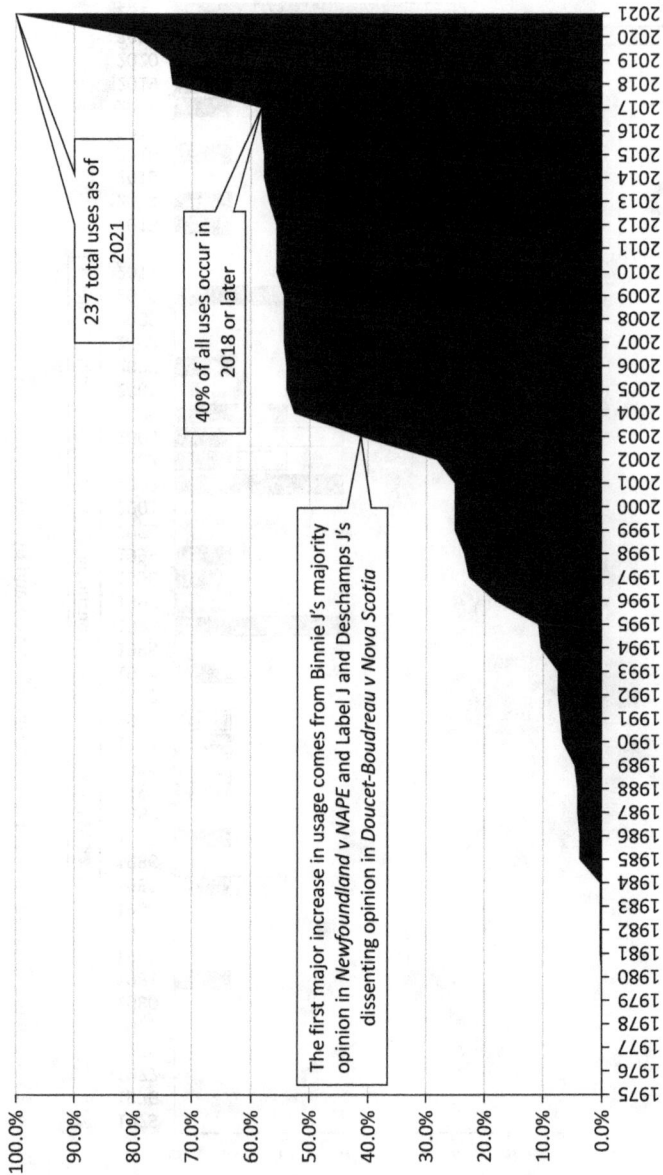

237 total uses as of 2021

40% of all uses occur in 2018 or later

The first major increase in usage comes from Binnie J's majority opinion in *Newfoundland v NAPE* and Label J and Deschamps J's dissenting opinion in *Doucet-Boudreau v Nova Scotia*

Figure 2.3 Cumulative uses of "Separation of Power" since 1975

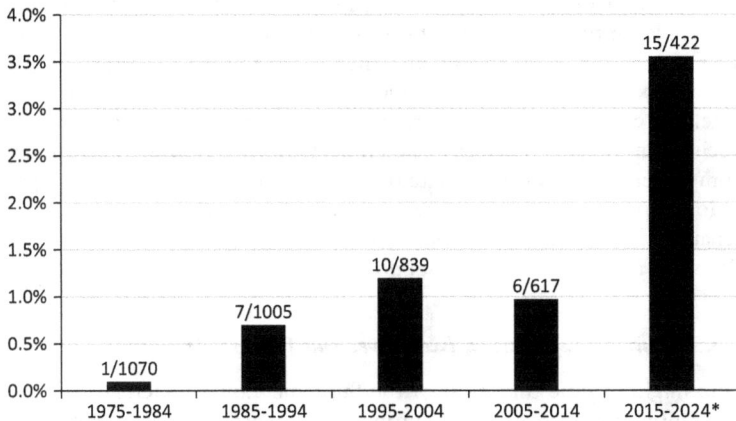

Figure 2.4 Separation of powers cases as a portion of all cases by decade

behind this trend, it is still possible to conclude that the Supreme Court is engaging with separation of powers issues explicitly and with some regularity. As we explain below, this is contributing to the development of a more robust conception of the separation of powers, as the principle is re-articulated and applied in a range of contexts.

2.3.2 Intellectual Leadership in Separation of Powers Cases

The second story is that Justices Karakatsanis, Brown, Rowe, and Côté are the justices on the Court who discuss the separation of powers most often in their decisions.[31] Justice Karakatsanis has authored the most majority opinions referencing the principle. Of the 13 majority opinions in which the separation of powers was mentioned since 2018, six were authored or co-authored by Justice Karakatsanis; three each by Justices Brown, Rowe, and Côté; two each by Chief Justice Wagner and Justice Martin; and one by Justice Gascon.[32] Of the concurring opinions, four were written by Justice Rowe and one each by Justices Karakatsanis, Brown, Abella, and Côté. Of the dissenting opinions, three were written by Justice Brown, three by Justice Côté, two by Justice Rowe, and one by Justice Karakatsanis.

---

31 Mathen et al. (this volume, Chapter 4).
32 Where an opinion was jointly authored, the opinion was attributed to each of the justices named as authors.

In short, the separation of powers is being invoked by a range of justices on the Court, but Justice Karakatsanis has emerged as an intellectual leader in the articulation of Canada's separation of powers doctrine. This appears to be true both in terms of the number of decisions she has authored, and the depth of the analysis her majority decisions provide. For example, she is the author of the majority opinion in the 2013 decision in *Ontario v Criminal Lawyers' Association of Ontario*, the most comprehensive treatment to date by a majority of the Court on the separation of powers.[33] She also appears to be the judge who can translate the separation of powers concerns of Justices Brown, Rowe, and Côte into decisions that attract majority support.

2.3.3 Securing Legislative, Executive, and Judicial Interests

One might assume that most of the Supreme Court's references to the separation of powers would occur in cases in which the Court concludes that a matter falls outside its purview; that is, as a way of declining jurisdiction in whole or in part. Indeed, this would be consistent with other, evolving trends in constitutional interpretation that tend to reflect a deferential posture towards the legislature.[34] However, this is not the story the case law tells. Of the 27 cases in which the majority or plurality has invoked the separation of powers to protect a specific branch, it secured the authority of the judicial branch in eight cases, the legislative branch in ten cases, and the executive in nine cases.[35]

Examining the terms that have been referenced alongside the separation of powers provides a second measure of the interests the Court is protecting in separation of powers cases. In 86% of cases in which the term "separation of power" appeared, the court also mentioned one or more of the following principles: parliamentary sovereignty, parliamentary supremacy, parliamentary privilege, judicial independence, the rule of law, and royal prerogative/"Crown's prerogative" (42 of 48 cases).[36] The

---

33 *Ontario v Criminal Lawyers' Association of Ontario*, 2013 SCC 43.
34 Vanessa MacDonnell, "The Enduring Wisdom of the Purposive Approach to *Charter* Interpretation" in Kerri Froc, Howard Kislowicz, and Richard Moon, eds, *The Surprising Constitution* (Vancouver: UBC Press, 2024 (forthcoming)).
35 A subset of the cases securing the authority of the executive dealt with prosecutorial discretion (3 cases): see *R v Anderson*, 2014 SCC 41; *Krieger v Law Society of Alberta*, 2002 SCC 65; *R v Power*, [1994] 1 SCR 601. Sometimes the Court invokes the separation of powers to protect more than one institution at a time. In *Canada v Alta Energy Luxembourg S.A.R.L.*, 2021 SCC 49, for example, the majority explained that "In accordance with the separation of powers, developing tax policy is the task of the executive and legislative branches": para. 96.
36 Schneiderman, *supra* note 1; Liston, *supra* note 4 at 12.

term appeared most often alongside "the rule of law", which was mentioned in 73% of the cases in our case set (35 of 48). The term "judicial independence" appeared in 25% of the cases (10 of 48). "Parliamentary sovereignty" was mentioned in 21% of the cases (10 of 48), while "parliamentary supremacy" appeared in 17% of cases (8 of 48). The terms "royal prerogative" or "Crown's prerogative" appeared in 27% of cases (13 of 48).

Keyness is a metric that shows how often words and phrases appear in proximity to a target word or phrase. We employed a keyness analysis to compare how often each of the selected principles was mentioned in opinions that discuss the separation of powers as compared to opinions that do not.[37] This allowed us to separate terms that are generally in frequent use from those that co-occur unusually often with "separation of power".

"Parliamentary privilege" is the highest-scoring term using this metric ($chi^2 = 8192$),[38] and is the term most likely to co-occur with "separation of power" across all terms in the dataset (i.e. all words, not just the selected principles). "Judicial independence" is a close second among the selected principles ($chi^2 = 5928$), and is the third most likely term to co-occur with "separation of power" overall, after "judges". Next is "parliamentary sovereignty" ($chi^2 = 1165$). "Rule of law" is more distantly connected using this metric ($chi^2 = 932$); although "rule of law" is frequently used in the same opinions as "separation of power", it is also used in a wide variety of other contexts and so scores lower on this metric. "Parliamentary supremacy" ($chi^2 = 127$) and "royal prerogative" ($chi^2 = 81$) are more distantly connected still. Oddly, "Crown's prerogative" is negatively correlated with "separation of powers" ($chi^2 = -221$), which indicates that it is less likely than the average word in our dataset to be used in the same opinion as "separation of power".

As a theoretical matter, the separation of powers can be understood as a true structural principle, one that does not prescribe particular outcomes *ex ante* or favour any one branch.[39] It should therefore produce

---

37 Due to limitations of our data, this analysis included only cases from 1975 to 2021.
38 Chi^2 is a metric that shows how likely an outcome is to occur, assuming that the underlying data is randomly distributed. Since language data is not randomly distributed, our chi^2 results cannot be used to calculate statistical significance. However, the comparative values allow for rank-ordering the degree of connection between terms. As a rough rule of thumb, chi^2 values above 1,000 can be considered indicative of a fair degree of connection between two terms. Values less than 100 indicate that the two terms are unlikely to be strongly connected. For further explanation, see Taylor, Charlotte, Anna Marchi, and Costas Gabrielatos, "Chapter 12: Keyness Analysis: Nature, Metrics and Techniques" in *Corpus Approaches to Discourse: A Critical Review* (Abingdon, Oxon: Routledge, 2018).
39 Liston, *supra* note 4.

outcomes that secure the spheres of action of the legislature, the executive, and the courts. This is borne out by the Supreme Court's application of the principle.

Of course, reference to the principle is at its most controversial when it is invoked to secure the jurisdiction of the Court itself. Indeed, Schneiderman suggests that the Court has made strategic use of the separation of powers to defend its own sphere of authority.[40] However, a review of the cases in which the Court has defended its own jurisdiction suggests that it has generally done so in ways that are consistent with separation of powers principles, in the sense that the intervention was designed to prevent encroachment by the other branches. There may be exceptions, of course: the *Judges Remuneration Reference* has been the subject of vociferous criticism for concluding that it would violate judicial independence for the political branches to decrease judges' salaries.[41] In the Reference, Chief Justice Lamer explained that "the institutional independence of the courts is inextricably bound up with the separation of powers, because in order to guarantee that the courts can protect the Constitution, they must be protected by a set of objective guarantees against intrusions by the executive and legislative branches of government".[42] To retain the Court's independence and impartiality, the majority concluded, it was essential that structures be put in place to prevent direct negotiation over salaries between the executive and the judiciary and ensure that the executive cannot meddle with judicial salaries.[43] Even in such a contested opinion, however, the Court was surely correct to identify the reduction of judicial salaries and judicial salary negotiations as a context in which the separation of powers and judicial independence might be vulnerable.

2.3.4 References to the Separation of Powers in Majority, Concurring, and Dissenting Judgments

A close reading of the cases suggests that while there was initial disagreement on the Court about the status of the separation of powers as a constitutional principle, the Court has largely coalesced around a common understanding of the concept. This common understanding is

---

40 Schneiderman, *supra* note 1.
41 Jean Leclair, "Canada's Unfathomable Unwritten Constitutional Principles" (2011) 27 Queen's LJ 389.
42 *Ref re Remuneration of Judges of the Prov Court of PEI; Ref re Independence and Impartiality of Judges of the Prov Court of PEI*, [1997] 3 SCR 3 at para. 139 [*Provincial Judges Reference*].
43 Leclair, *supra* note 38.

perhaps best reflected in the majority's decision in *Ontario v Criminal Lawyers' Association*, decided in 2013. The case provides one of the more detailed accounts of the separation of powers in Canada, and has been cited repeatedly since 2013 for that reason.[44] The case stands for four main propositions. The first is that "[Canada's] constitutional framework prescribes different roles for the executive, legislative and judicial branches".[45] The second is that these distinct roles have evolved over time, and that each branch of state is recognized to have certain "core competencies".[46] Third, each branch must respect the core competencies of the other branches, and refrain from "interfering" in their affairs.[47] And fourth, in areas of shared jurisdiction, institutions should be cautious about exercising authority that is perhaps more appropriately exercised by another branch.[48]

While scholars are therefore correct to suggest that for decades the Court's statements about the separation of powers were "skeletal", the jurisprudence of the last decade has articulated the contours of the principle with increasing detail.[49] Canada's modern separation of powers doctrine, as articulated in *Ontario v CLA* and re-iterated in *City of Toronto, Mikisew Cree, Nelson (City) v Marchi* and *British Columbia (Attorney General) v Provincial Court Judges' Association of British Columbia*, embraces the idea that each branch of state has particular competencies, and that these competencies should be respected by the other branches.[50] This version of the principle has much in common with Newman's account of the separation of powers as involving a form of constitutional equilibrium. It also resonates strongly with Kavanagh's theoretical rendering of the separation of powers, which emphasizes inter-branch "comity" and "collaboration."[51]

As noted above, the Court was unanimous in one third of the cases studied. In the remaining cases, the Court divided, and our reading shows that in 58% of those cases, one of the reasons for the division was disagreement over how the separation of powers applies to the facts before

44 *References re Greenhouse Gas Pollution Pricing Act, supra* note 26 Cote J, dissenting.

45 *Ontario v Criminal Lawyers' Association of Ontario, supra* note 32 at para. 27.

46 Ibid. at paras 27–28.

47 Ibid. at para. 29.

48 Ibid. at para. 31.

49 Liston, *supra* note 4. See also Newman, *supra* note 5.

50 As noted, one important case that discusses the separation of powers at some length without actually using the term is *New Brunswick Broadcasting Co. v Nova Scotia (Speaker of the House of Assembly), supra* note 25. It articulates the basic principles in much the same way as the cases listed above.

51 Aileen Kavanagh, "Recasting the Political Constitution: From Rivals to Relationships" (2019) 30:1 King's Law Journal 43; Kavanagh, *supra* note 1.

them (19 out of 32 cases).[52] This suggests that the Court is still struggling to apply this principle in concrete contexts.

Disagreements regarding the application of the separation of powers principle can take a variety of forms. For example, in *Toronto (City) v Ontario (Attorney General)*, the majority and the dissent divided on the question of whether unwritten constitutional principles are capable of invalidating legislation.[53] The majority stated that it would violate the separation of powers for judges to rely on unwritten principles to strike down legislation.[54] The dissent thought that it was within courts' power to enforce these principles when they are infringed by legislation. In the *Greenhouse Gas Pollution Pricing Reference*, Justice Côté dissented from the majority's reasons, which upheld a Henry VIII clause in the federal *Greenhouse Gas Pollution Pricing Act*.[55] A Henry VIII clause permits the executive to alter the content of primary legislation through the promulgation of regulations.[56] Côté concluded that this type of arrangement violated the separation of powers and other unwritten constitutional principles.[57] The majority did not address these arguments. And in *Ontario v Criminal Lawyers' Association of Ontario*, the issue was whether, in ordering the appointment of an *amicus curiae*, a court should also be permitted to set the salary that would be paid by the Ministry of the Attorney General, or whether doing so interfered with financial matters best left to the executive. The majority concluded that determining the salary of an *amicus* would exceed the judicial function and be in tension with the separation of powers. The dissent saw no conflict and would have upheld the trial judge's decision to set the salary.

These doctrinal divisions may reflect a tension inherent in the application of the separation of powers principle. It is one thing to agree on the importance of respecting the institutional competencies of the different branches of state, and of maintaining a constitutional equilibrium; it is another thing to draw such lines in concrete cases, particularly since the doctrine continues to rely on a definition of the separation of powers

---

52 This assessment was made by reading each decision in which the Court split, and assessing whether the separation of powers appeared to provide a basis for the division. On disagreement, see generally Mathen et al. (this volume, Chapter 4).

53 *Toronto (City) v Ontario (Attorney General)*, 2021 SCC 34.

54 Ibid. at para. 56.

55 SC 2018, c 12.

56 *References re Greenhouse Gas Pollution Pricing Act, supra* note 26; Paul Daly, "The Constitutionality of Henry VIII Clauses in Canada: Administrative Law Matter (No. 1) in the *References re Greenhouse Gas Pollution Pricing Act, 2021 SCC 11*", (April 22, 2021), online: *Administrative Law Matters* https://www.administrativelawmatters.com/blog/2021/04/22/the-constitutionality-of-henry-viii-clauses-in-canada-administrative-law-matter-no-1-in-the-references-re-greenhouse-gas-pollution-pricing-act-2021-scc-11/.

57 *References re Greenhouse Gas Pollution Pricing Act, supra* note 26 at para. 222.

that downplays the extent of the functional overlap that exists in practice. The Court is likely to continue to struggle, and sometimes disagree, on where those lines should be drawn. There will be better and worse examples of the application of the doctrine. In the aggregate, however, the Court's decisions evince a commitment to inter-institutional respect and constitutional equilibrium, values which Kavanagh and Newman identify as central to the separation of powers.[58]

2.4 Conclusion

The separation of powers is now a frequently cited concept in the case law, in both constitutional and non-constitutional cases. The data from 2021, showing that the principle was invoked in one fifth of cases in which the Court issued a written decision, indicates that the principle is playing an important role in the Supreme Court's jurisprudence. This trend is not limited to a few judges or to judges who are normally in dissent, though Justice Karakatsanis has emerged as the current leading voice in articulating the contours of the doctrine.

Our review of the cases makes it possible to conclude that Canada does, in fact, have a separation of powers doctrine. According to the Court, the principle is concerned with maintaining what Newman refers to as a "constitutional equilibrium" between branches of state. It is a principle that may require the Court to protect its own sphere of authority, or to hold back in whole or in part in deference to the political branches, depending on the circumstances. To date, the principle does appear to be operating this way: as a structural constitutional principle that does not systematically favour one institution over others, but rather seeks to advance the tenets of "comity" and "collaboration," two features Kavanagh identifies as being central to a well-functioning constitutional order.

This chapter has sought to provide an initial sketch of Canada's separation of powers doctrine through an exercise in systematic analysis. Further research can and should be pursued on some of the second-order questions raised by our findings. Among other things, it would be interesting to know why references to the separation of powers seem to be increasing. It would also be helpful to examine whether there is empirical support for Schneiderman's suggestion that the Court has deployed the separation of powers principle strategically to secure its own authority. And it would be important to further investigate what is driving disagreement among members of the Court regarding the application of the principle in concrete cases. At a conceptual level, there is room for more

---

58 Kavanagh, *supra* note 1; Newman, *supra* note 5.

research on whether the separation of powers has staying power as a constitutional principle given some of the tensions inherent in the principle that this chapter and other works have identified.

In our view, some version of the separation of powers is likely to remain salient given that constitutionalism is increasingly understood as being a whole-of-state project. In an era marked by increasing mistrust of politicians, the consolidation of executive power, and wariness about courts, theories of inter-branch coordination are increasingly useful in explaining how constitutional democracies operate as interdependent systems.[59] The devil, of course, is in the details. The hard work lies in articulating a theory of the separation of powers that actually works: that is descriptively accurate, and that is normatively a good fit with Canada's constitutional order.

---

59 Rouleau Commission Report, online: https://publicorderemergencycommission.ca/final -report/.

Appendix A: Uses of "Separation of Power" since 1975 by Opinion Type[60]

Year	Case Title	# of Uses by Opinion Maj	Con	Dis	2+ Opinions	Unanimous
2022	Society of Composers, Authors and Music Publishers of Canada v. Entertainment Software Association	1	0			
2022	R. v. Bisonnette	1				✓
2022	R. v. Sharma	2		2	✓	
2022	Anderson v. Alberta	3				✓
2021	Canada v. Alta Energy Luxembourg S.A.R.L	1		0		
2021	R. v. Albashir	4		0		
2021	R. v. Parranto		1	0		
2021	Nelson (City) v. Marchi	12				✓
2021	Toronto (City) v. Ontario (Attorney General)	4		0		
2021	Reference re Code of Civil Procedure (Que.), art. 35	1		0		
2021	R. v. Chouhan		6	0		
2021	References re Greenhouse Gas Pollution Pricing Act	0		20	✓	
2020	Ontario (Attorney General) v. G	1	0	0		
2020	British Columbia (Attorney General) v. Provincial Court Judges' Association of British Columbia	4				✓
2020	Nevsun Resources Ltd. v. Araya	0		8	✓	
2019	Desgagnés Transport Inc. v. Wärtsilä Canada Inc.	1	0			
2018	Mikisew Cree First Nation v. Canada (Governor General in Council)		31		✓	
2018	Chagnon v. Syndicat de la fonction publique et parapublique du Québec	3	1	1	✓	
2016	Conférence des juges de paix magistrats du Québec v. Quebec (Attorney General)	1				✓
2014	R. v. Anderson	2				✓
2013	Ontario v. Criminal Lawyers' Association of Ontario	3		0		
2010	R. v. Conway	2				✓
2010	Canada (Prime Minister) v. Khadr	1				✓
2007	Canada (Attorney General) v. Hislop	1	0			
2006	Reference re Employment Insurance Act (Can.), ss. 22 and 23	1				✓
2005	Canada (House of Commons) v. Vaid	2				✓
2004	Newfoundland (Treasury Board) v. N.A.P.E.	22				✓
2004	Application under s. 83. 28 of the Criminal Code (Re)		0	4		
2004	Canadian Foundation for Children, Youth and the Law v. Canada (Attorney General)	0		1		
2003	Doucet-Boudreau v. Nova Scotia (Minister of Education)	1		30	✓	
2002	Krieger v. Law Society of Alberta	2				✓
2002	Babcock v. Canada (Attorney General)	2	0			
2002	Mackin v. New Brunswick (Minister of Finance); Rice v. New Brunswick	3		0		
1999	Wells v. Newfoundland	4				✓
1998	Reference re Secession of Quebec	2				✓
1997	Ref re Remuneration of Judges of the Prov. Court of P.E.I	11		0		
1996	Cooper v. Canada (Human Rights Commission)	0	14	0		
1996	Harvey v. New Brunswick (Attorney General)	1	2		✓	
1995	MacMillan Bloedel Ltd. v. Simpson	0		1		
1994	R. v. Power	7		0		
1992	Thomson v. Canada (Deputy Minister of Agriculture)	0		1		
1991	Committee for the Commonwealth of Canada v. Canada		1			
1990	Douglas/kwantlen Faculty Assn. v. Douglas College		5			
1989	Sobeys Stores Ltd. v. Yeomans and Labour Standards Tribunal (N.S.)	1	0			
1987	Ontario (Attorney General) v. OPSEU	1	0			
1986	Fraser v. P.S.S.R.B	1				✓
1985	Operation Dismantle v. The Queen	0	7			
1981	Re Residential Tenancies Act	1				✓

Figure A2.1

60 In cases where "separation of power" was mentioned in multiple opinions of the same type, this table adds those uses together (e.g. the four concurrences in *Mikisew Cree* use the term a total of 20 times). The column "2+ Opinions" indicates cases in which the term was used in more than one opinion.

Appendix B: Opinions Using the Term "Separation of Power" Since 1975

Year	Case Title	Opinion Author	Opinion Type	# of Uses of "Separation of Power"
2022	*Society of Composers, Authors and Music Publishers of Canada v. Entertainment Software Association*	Rowe J	Majority	1
2022	*R. v. Bissonnette*	Wagner CJ	Majority	1
2022	*R. v. Sharma*	Brown & Rowe JJ	Majority	2
2022	*R. v. Sharma*	Karakatsanis J	Dissenting	2
2022	*Anderson v. Alberta*	Karakatsanis & Brown JJ	Majority	3
2021	*Canada v. Alta Energy Luxembourg S.A.R.L.*	Côté J	Majority	1
2021	*R. v. Albashir*	Karakatsanis J	Majority	4
2021	*R. v. Parranto*	Rowe J	Concurring	1
2021	*Nelson (City) v. Marchi*	Karakatsanis & Martin JJ	Majority	12
2021	*Toronto (City) v. Ontario (Attorney General)*	Wagner CJ & Brown J	Majority	4
2021	*Reference re Code of Civil Procedure (Que.), art. 35*	Côté & Martin JJ	Majority	1
2021	*R. v. Chouhan*	Rowe J	Concurring	6
2021	*References re Greenhouse Gas Pollution Pricing Act*	Côté J	Dissenting	19
2021	*References re Greenhouse Gas Pollution Pricing Act*	Brown J	Dissenting	1
2020	*Ontario (Attorney General) v. G*	Karakatsanis J	Majority	1
2020	*British Columbia (Attorney General) v. Provincial Court Judges' Association of British Columbia*	Karakatsanis J	Majority	4
2020	*Nevsun Resources Ltd. v. Araya*	Brown & Rowe JJ	Dissenting	3
2020	*Nevsun Resources Ltd. v. Araya*	Côté J	Dissenting	5
2019	*Desgagnés Transport Inc. v. Wärtsilä Canada Inc.*	Côté Rowe & Gascon JJ	Majority	1

Year	Case Title	Opinion Author	Opinion Type	# of Uses of "Separation of Power"
2018	*Mikisew Cree First Nation v. Canada (Governor General in Council)*	Karakatsanis J	Concurring	10
2018	*Mikisew Cree First Nation v. Canada (Governor General in Council)*	Abella J	Concurring	2
2018	*Mikisew Cree First Nation v. Canada (Governor General in Council)*	Brown J	Concurring	11
2018	*Mikisew Cree First Nation v. Canada (Governor General in Council)*	Rowe J	Concurring	8
2018	*Chagnon v. Syndicat de la fonction publique et parapublique du Québec*	Karakatsanis J	Majority	3
2018	*Chagnon v. Syndicat de la fonction publique et parapublique du Québec*	Rowe	Concurring	1
2018	*Chagnon v. Syndicat de la fonction publique et parapublique du Québec*	Côté & Brown JJ	Dissenting	1
2016	*Conférence des juges de paix magistrats du Québec v. Quebec (Attorney General)*	Wagner CJ, Karakatsanis & Côté JJ	Majority	1

Year	Case Title	Opinion Author	Opinion Type	# of Uses of "Separation of Power"
2014	*R. v. Anderson*	Moldaver J	Majority	2
2013	*Ontario v. Criminal Lawyers' Association of Ontario*	Karakatsanis J	Majority	3
2010	*R. v. Conway*	Abella J	Majority	2
2010	*Canada (Prime Minister) v. Khadr*	The Court	Majority	1
2007	*Canada (Attorney General) v. Hislop*	Rothstein & Lebel JJ	Majority	1
2005	*Reference re Employment Insurance Act (Can.), ss. 22 and 23*	Deschamps J	Majority	1

Year	Case Title	Opinion Author	Opinion Type	# of Uses of "Separation of Power"
2005	*Canada (House of Commons) v. Vaid*	Binnie J	Majority	2
2034	*Newfoundland (Treasury Board) v. N.A.P.E.*	Binnie J	Majority	22
2034	*Application under s. 83.28 of the Criminal Code (Re)*	Lebel J	Dissenting	4
2034	*Canadian Foundation for Children, Youth and the Law v. Canada (Attorney General)*	Deschamps J	Dissenting	1
2003	*Doucet-Boudreau v. Nova Scotia (Minister of Education)*	Iacobucci & Arbour JJ	Majority	1
2003	*Doucet-Boudreau v. Nova Scotia (Minister of Education)*	Lebel & Deschamps JJ	Dissenting	30
2032	*Krieger v. Law Society of Alberta*	Major & Iacobucci JJ	Majority	2
2002	*Babcock v. Canada (Attorney General)*	McLachlin CJ	Majority	2
2002	*Mackin v. New Brunswick (Minister of Finance); Rice v. New Brunswick*	Gonthier J	Majority	3
1999	*Wells v. Newfoundland*	Major J	Majority	4
1998	*Reference re Secession of Quebec*	The Court	Majority	2
1997	*Ref re Remuneration of Judges of the Prov. Court of P.E.I.*	Lamer CJ	Majority	11
1996	*Cooper v. Canada (Human Rights Commission)*	Lamer CJ	Concurring	14
1996	*Harvey v. New Brunswick (Attorney General)*	La Forest J	Majority	1
1996	*Harvey v. New Brunswick (Attorney General)*	McLachlin J	Concurring	2
1995	*MacMillan Bloedel Ltd. v. Simpson*	McLachlin J	Dissenting	1
1994	*R. v. Power*	L'Heureux-Dubé J	Majority	7
1992	*Thomson v. Canada (Deputy Minister of Agriculture)*	L'Heureux-Dubé J	Dissenting	1
1991	*Committee for the Commonwealth of Canada v. Canada*	Lamer CJ	Concurring	1

Year	Case Title	Opinion Author	Opinion Type	# of Uses of "Separation of Power"
1990	*Douglas/kwantlen Faculty Assn. v. Douglas College*	La Forest J	Concurring	5
1989	*Sobeys Stores Ltd. v. Yeomans and Labour Standards Tribunal (N.S.)*	Wilson J	Majority	1
1987	*Ontario (Attorney General) v. OPSEU*	Beetz J	Majority	1
1985	Fraser v. P.S.S.R.B.	Dickson CJ	Majority	1
1985	*Operation Dismantle v. The Queen*	Wilson J	Concurring	7
1981	*Re Residential Tenancies Act*	Dickson CJ	Majority	1

3 Using Network Citation Analysis to Reveal Precedential Archetypes at the Supreme Court of Canada

Wolfgang Alschner[1] and Isabelle St-Hilaire[2]

3.1 Introduction

The doctrine of precedent – the notion that courts rely on previous decisions to settle the disputes that come before them[3] – underpins the judicial reasoning of Supreme Court justices and ensures that Canadian law develops through a series of analogies with and distinctions from earlier cases. Citations through which later decisions engage with earlier ones are the most explicit manifestations of precedent at work. Legal scholars, political scientists, and practitioners have long been drawn to citation patterns to study the rise and fall of precedents. As this chapter will show, however, a network analysis perspective combined with natural language processing tools improves the ability of researchers to gain insights from citations.

Raw citation counts can be misleading on several fronts. Raw counts overestimate the importance of precedents in high-volume litigation areas that attract many references but do not leave much of a mark on broader jurisprudence. Conversely, raw counts underestimate the enduring influence of early cases that attract few direct citations but that shaped subsequent landmark decisions that continue to be widely cited. Finally, raw counts neglect what matters most to lawyers – do later decisions in fact *follow* earlier ones? Indeed, when a case overrules a prior case,

---

1 University of Ottawa; wolfgang.alschner@uottawa.ca. ORCID: 0000-0003-4744-1404. We gratefully acknowledge the research assistance of Gareth Spanglett, as well as the background research by Sonia Anand Knowlton and Thomas Boyd.
2 DPhil student at the University of Oxford. ORCID: 0000-0002-9578-0307.
3 See, for example, Iain Carmichael et al., "Examining the Evolution of Legal Precedent through Citation Network Analysis" (2017) 96 NCL Rev 227 at 228.

DOI: 10.4324/9781003279112-5

it terminates that precedent's authority – yet raw citation counts would treat the overruling citation as yet another supporting reference.

Legal data analytics can mitigate these shortcomings. Network analysis places a decision in the wider web of cross-citations, which helps distinguish between highly cited peripheral cases and core landmark decisions. Furthermore, it captures the indirect influence a precedent still exerts even when it is cited less frequently. For its part, natural language processing helps to tease out how precedent is used in subsequent cases by distinguishing between positive and negative citations.

This chapter first discusses existing citation analyses of the Supreme Court of Canada (SCC) and then contrasts them with more recent legal data analytics approaches applied to other apex courts. The final segment of the chapter then applies network analysis and natural language processing to identify precedential archetypes based on 9,295 cross-citations between SCC constitutional cases since 1983. These archetypes represent different trajectories or life cycles of SCC precedents, from the "eternal star" that is cited consistently and widely to the "displaced pioneer" that is overtaken, but not overruled, by subsequent jurisprudence.

Identifying such archetypes is useful for several reasons. First, by distinguishing between varying life cycles, archetypes unpack the notion of leading cases and reveal their underlying diversity. Second, archetypes facilitate the comparative study of precedents and focus the debate on the determinants of success and failure of precedents across subject areas. Third, archetypes are useful teaching tools that highlight the variable fates and uncertain futures of individual cases and the role they play in specific areas of law. Finally, archetypes can help courts and litigants to weigh precedent-based arguments against a precedent's life cycle and its placement in the wider jurisprudential network.

3.2 Citation Analyses of the Supreme Court of Canada

Scholars have long studied the Supreme Court and its evolving case law through quantitative citation analyses for both conceptual and practical reasons. Conceptually, citations are generally thought to matter.[4] As Peter McCormick puts it, "judges do not cite earlier decisions casually [...] Citation involves selection, and that selection sends a signal, and

---

4 The role of citations can vary considerably amongst courts, with some, such as the Court of Justice of the European Union, using them in a more ritualistic than argumentative fashion. See Karen McAuliffe, "Precedent at the Court of Justice of the European Union: The Linguistic Aspect" in Michael Freeman and Fiona Smith, eds, *Law and Language: Current Legal Issues*, 2013) 483. In contrast, in common law courts, where precedent and reasoning around precedent play a more foundational role, judges are less likely to cite casually.

the changing patterns of those signals convey information".[5] Practically, citations are easily countable. They thus provide a readily available and quantifiable proxy for the otherwise elusive concept of precedent.

Researchers have studied the Supreme Court's citation patterns to empirically trace normative and institutional change at the Court. The Charter era has been a focus of attention. McCormick noted that decisions tend to be cited less and less frequently over time.[6] He then compared the half-life of citations between Chief Justiceships. He found that decisions in the Dickson Court predominantly referenced recent precedents whereas older citations with an average half-life of more than 17 years dominated in the post-2006 McLachlin Court. To McCormick, this suggested an important jurisprudential shift from a "Charter revolution" under Dickson to a "settled case law" under McLachlin.[7]

Another focus of citation analysis has been the use of jurisprudence borrowed from United States' courts by the SCC. A range of studies have tracked references to US case law to gauge the role of American case law in the Supreme Court of Canada's jurisprudence.[8] Collectively, these studies found a modest reliance by the SCC on US law, which peaked in the early days of the Charter and has been decreasing since.

Although this literature underscores the potential that citation analysis exhibits for the study of courts and jurisprudential change, it also raises questions as to how much significance scholars can and should accord to raw citation data.

---

5 Peter J. McCormick, *The End of the Charter Revolution: Looking Back from the New Normal* (Toronto, University of Toronto Press, 2014) at 200. We acknowledge that there is "noise" in that signal since citations may occur on the initiative of different stakeholders (e.g. judges, clerks, litigants). However, they ultimately need to be sanctioned by the justices. See Kelly Bodwin, Jeffrey S. Rosenthal, and Albert H. Yoon, "Opinion Writing and Authorship on the Supreme Court of Canada" (2013) 63:2 UTLJ 159.

6 McCormick, *supra* note 5 at 203–207.

7 *Ibid.*

8 Christopher P Manfredi, "The Use of United States Decisions by the Supreme Court of Canada under the Charter of Rights and Freedoms" (1990) 23:3 Can J Political Science 499; Gerard V. La Forest, "The Use of American Precedents in Canadian Courts" (1994) 46:2 Main L Rev 211; C.L. Ostberg, Matthew E. Wetstein, and Craig R. Ducat, "Attitudes, Precedents and Cultural Change: Explaining the Citation of Foreign Precedents by the Supreme Court of Canada" (2001) 34:2 Can J Political Science 377; Bijon Roy, "An Empirical Survey of Foreign Jurisprudence and International Instruments in Charter Litigation" (2004) 62:22 UT Fac L Rev 99; Peter McCormick, "American Citations and the McLachlin Court: An Empirical Study" (2009) 47:1 Osgoode Hall LJ 83; Klodian Rado, "The Judicial Diplomacy of the Supreme Court of Canada and Its Impact: An Empirical Overview" (2020) 58:1 Alta L Rev 1.

3.3 From Citation Counts to Network Measures

Citations by themselves are an imperfect proxy for studying the normative importance and influence of a case for three principal reasons. First, and most obviously, a case may be cited for different propositions, which then trigger very different normative consequences. A case can be referenced as a precedent to be followed, bolstering its normative importance. But a citation may also be used to distinguish a prior case from the present one, to overrule an earlier precedent, or to note in passing other decisions dealing with similar issues. As Hitt notes, "measuring all citations, positive, negative, and neutral, may mistakenly count[ ] some criticisms as legal influence".[9] As a result, researchers need to distinguish between citation types to accurately gauge the normative role of a citation.

Second, not all citations, even if they are positive, signal equal importance. *Dunsmuir*, for example, is by far the most cited SCC judgment in Canadian courts.[10] Yet, while *Dunsmuir* is widely considered a landmark judgment, its pre-eminence over other important SCC decisions in overall citation counts results from the fact that, for over a decade, nearly every administrative law case implicated the standard of review analysis it coined. More generally, a case that settles a recurring question in a highly litigated area of the law will by necessity become highly cited, but these citations tell us little about that cases' broader normative relevance for other areas of jurisprudence. Raw citation counts may therefore reflect the *practical* importance of a case, but not necessarily its *normative* role in the larger edifice of Canadian law.[11] It is thus important to distinguish between highly cited, but peripheral cases, and highly cited central cases that shaped diverse areas of law.

Third, while references to a case may decline, its jurisprudential influence may linger. The common law has famously been likened to a chain novel.[12] The metaphor suggests a path-dependency that underscores the crucial importance of earlier cases: they set the course for subsequent legal developments.[13] While the case law may evolve away from them over time, the link to earlier cases typically remains unbroken, rare instances of

9 Matthew P. Hitt, "Measuring Precedent in a Judicial Hierarchy" (2016) 50:1 Law & Soc'y Rev 57, 67.

10 Robert Danay, "*Dunsmuir* Focus Feature: Introduction" (2019) 69:1 UTLJ 1.

11 In that vein, Neale found that raw citation counts correlate closely with the number of page views the case received from users on CanLII. Thom Neale, "Citation Analysis of Canadian Case Law" (2013) 1:1 J Open Access to L 1, 23.

12 Ronald Dworkin, *Law's Empire* (Cambridge, MA: Harvard University Press, 1986).

13 Oona A. Hathaway, "Path Dependence in the Law: The Course and Pattern of Legal Change in a Common Law System" (2001) 86:2 Iowa L Rev 601.

overruled precedents notwithstanding. The absence of citations to a prior case may thus obfuscate the continuous influence that the case still exerts.

This latter point is well illustrated by the role early US precedents played in the development of Charter jurisprudence. Although Chief Justice Dickson noted that the SCC sought to develop a "distinctively Canadian approach" to the newly enacted Charter,[14] he also acknowledged the influence of these decisions: "[w]hile we must, of course, be wary of adopting American interpretations where they do not accord with the interpretive framework of our Constitution, the American courts have the benefit of two hundred years of experience in constitutional interpretation. This wealth of experience may offer guidance to the judiciary in this country."[15]

As Charter jurisprudence developed and evolved, references to American case law, initially frequent in Charter cases, declined even as their normative impact continued. Consider the development of a right to a speedy trial. The Canadian equivalent to the US Constitution's Sixth Amendment is s. 11(b) of the Charter, which provides that any person charged with an offence has the right to be tried within a reasonable time.[16] In an early Charter case, *R v Askov*, the Dickson Court set out the criteria for whether an accused's right has been infringed.[17] *Askov* built upon previous s. 11(b) cases, which included *Mills v The Queen* (1986),[18] *R v Rahey* (1987),[19] and *R v Conway* (1989).[20] On its face, *Askov* only considers the American case of *Barker v Wingo*.[21] However, *Mills* and *Rahey*, in turn, relied on two additional American Sixth Amendment cases, *Ewell*[22] and *Strunk*.[23]

The American jurisprudence influencing the *Askov* s. 11(b) framework is thus partly obscured if one looks at raw citations, but it becomes visible once the broader citation network is considered (Figure 3.1). Networks

---

14 Robert J. Sharpe and Kent Roach, *Brian Dickson: A Judge's Journey* (Toronto: University of Toronto Press for the Osgoode Society for Legal History, 2003) at 317.

15 *R v Simmons*, [1988] 2 SCR 495 at 516, 55 DLR (4th) 673, cited in Ostberg, Wetstein, and Ducat, *supra* note 8 at 381.

16 "Section 11(b) – Trial within a Reasonable Time" (last modified April 14, 2022), online: *Department of Justice*, www.justice.gc.ca/eng/csj-sjc/rfc-dlc/ccrf-ccdl/check/art11b .html.

17 *R v Askov*, [1990] 2 SCR 1199, 74 DLR (4th) 355 [*Askov*].

18 [1986] 1 SCR 863, 29 DLR (4th) 161 [*Mills*].

19 [1987] 1 SCR 588, 39 DLR (4th) 481 [*Rahey*].

20 [1989] 1 SCR 1659, 96 NR 241 [*Conway*].

21 407 US 514 (1972) [*Wingo*].

22 *United States v Ewell*, 383 US 116 (1966) [*Ewell*].

23 *Strunk v United States*, 412 US 434 (1973) [*Strunk*].

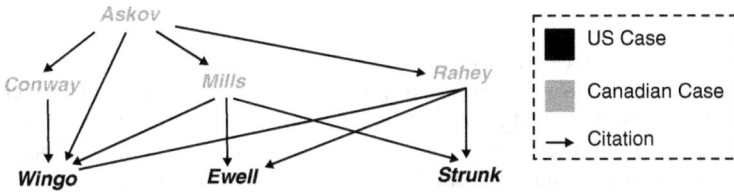

Figure 3.1 The citation network underlying the early Charter jurisprudence on the right to a speedy trial

are composed of nodes and links between these nodes.[24] Here, the nodes are decisions while the links are citations – references in one decision pointing to another. Legal citation networks are directional: if *Askov* cites *Conway*, it is an "outward citation" for *Askov* and an "inward citation" for *Conway*.[25]

In short, raw counts of citations are imperfect proxies of the normative influence of a precedent. They can produce exaggerated, understated, or misleading interpretations of the importance of cases. As illustrated below, it is here that network analysis, combined with natural language processing, comes in. Natural language processing can help differentiate between types of citations, separating cases that follow precedent from those that distinguish or overrule it. In addition, network analysis can place citations in their wider jurisprudential context, making it possible to separate central from peripheral cases and capture the networked conceptualization of case law implicit in the chain novel metaphor.

Scholars in other jurisdictions have recognized this potential of network analysis and used it to study various apex courts. This includes the Supreme Court of the United States[26] and the Italian Supreme Court,[27] as well as a range of international courts.[28] Thom Neale used net-

---

24 See James H. Fowler and Sangick Jeon, "The Authority of Supreme Court Precedent" (2008) 30:1 Soc Networks 16 at 17–18. Nodes are also referred to as vertices and edges as arcs.
25 *Ibid* at 18.
26 Fowler and Jeon, *supra* note 24; James H. Fowler et al., "Network Analysis and the Law: Measuring the Legal Importance of Precedents at the U.S. Supreme Court" (2007) 15:3 Political Analysis 324; Yonatan Lupu and James H. Fowler, "Strategic Citations to Precedent on the US Supreme Court" (2013) 42:1 J Leg Stud 151.
27 Tommaso Agnoloni and Ugo Pagallo, "The Case Law of the Italian Constitutional Court, Its Power Laws, and the Web of Scholarly Opinions" (Proceedings of the 15th International Conference on Artificial Intelligence and Law, San Diego, June 8, 2015).
28 Yonatan Lupu and Erik Voeten, "Precedent in International Courts: A Network Analysis of Case Citations by the European Court of Human Rights" (2012) 42:2 British J

work analysis to investigate citations to the Supreme Court among all other Canadian citations.[29] While technically advanced and cleverly implemented, his analysis focused on the structural and methodological aspects of the network rather than the ebb and flow of precedent.

The study most analogous to this chapter was carried out by Fowler and Jeon, who looked at the authority of precedent before the Supreme Court of the United States.[30] They found that overruled cases continued to be influential and that the Court's priorities visibly shifted as some areas of the law settled while others developed. They also compared the rise and fall of individual precedents. They observed, for example, that *Brown v Board of Education*, which deemed racial segregation at schools unconstitutional and which was highly controversial in the American South, took many years to attract citations and gain a central status in the citation network, whereas *Roe v Wade* became a landmark decision that was central to the network in just a few years.

The insight that landmark cases lead very different lives motivates the remainder of this chapter. In the next section, we apply Fowler and Jeon's methods to the Supreme Court of Canada's jurisprudence to show how data analytics can reveal different precedential archetypes, which provide a more nuanced view of the rising and falling influence of landmark cases.

3.4 Dataset and Methodology

Our analysis focuses on citations of SCC cases from 1983 to 2021. As noted above and highlighted in Chapter 2, the 1982 Charter revolutionized Canadian constitutional law and produced its most important precedents. We therefore concentrated on the modern, post-Charter Court and the almost 4,000 decisions rendered in this period. We identified over 41,000 cross-references to other SCC cases in these decisions, which we trimmed down to 11,115 to focus on cross-citations between constitutional cases only, defined as those that use the term "constitutional law" in one of the case headnotes.

We then excluded all dissenting opinions and focused only on majority opinions. To account for different types of citations, we further inspected the headnotes in SCC decisions that enumerate the cited decisions by

---

Political Science 413; Mattias Derlén and Johan Lindholm, "Goodbye *van Gend en Loos*, Hello *Bosman*? Using Network Analysis to Measure the Importance of Individual CJEU Judgments" (2014) 20:5 Eur LJ 667; Joost Pauwelyn, "Minority Rules: Precedent and Participation Before the WTO Appellate Body" in Joanna Jemielniak, Laura Nielsen, and Henrik Palmer Olsen, eds, *Establishing Judicial Authority in International Economic Law* (Cambridge, UK: Cambridge University Press 2016) 141.

29 Neale, *supra* note 11.
30 Fowler and Jeon, *supra* note 24.

Cases Cited

By LeBel J.

Applied: *R. v. Cheddesingh*, [2004] 1 S.C.R. 433, 2004 SCC 16; **distinguished:** *R. v. M.P.*, [2005] Q.J. No. 78 (QL), 2005 QCCA 7; **referred to:** *R. v. Shropshire*, 1995 CanLII 47 (SCC), [1995] 4 S.C.R. 227; *R. v. McDonnell*, 1997 CanLII 389 (SCC), [1997] 1 S.C.R. 948; *R. v. M. (C.A.)*, 1996 CanLII 230 (SCC), [1996] 1 S.C.R. 500; *R. v. W. (G.)*, 1999 CanLII 668 (SCC), [1999] 3 S.C.R. 597; *R. v. Johnson*, [2003] 2 S.C.R. 357, 2003 SCC 46; *R. v. Proulx*, [2000] 1 S.C.R. 61, 2000 SCC 5; *R. v. Lyons*, 1987 CanLII 25 (SCC), [1987] 2 S.C.R. 309; *R. v. Jones*, 1994 CanLII 85 (SCC), [1994] 2 S.C.R. 229; *Beaulieu v. R.*, [2007] Q.J. No. 2116 (QL), 2007 QCCA 403; *Corneau v. R.*, 2001 CanLII 20599 (QC CA), [2001] R.J.Q. 2509; *R. v. Ménard*, [2002] Q.J. No. 5271 (QL); *R. v. M. (J.S.)* (2003), 173 C.C.C. (3d) 75, 2003 BCCA 66; *R. v. Archer* (2005), 2005 CanLII 1621 (ON CA), 193 C.C.C. (3d) 376; *R. v. Blair* (2002), 167 B.C.A.C. 21, 2002 BCCA 205; *R. v. J.G.E.S.*, [2006] B.C.J. No. 3455 (QL), 2006 BCSC 2004.

By Fish J. (dissenting)

R. v. M. (C.A.), 1996 CanLII 230 (SCC), [1996] 1 S.C.R. 500; *R. v. Shropshire*, 1995 CanLII 47 (SCC), [1995] 4 S.C.R. 227; *R. v. Larche*, [2006] 2 S.C.R. 762, 2006 SCC 56.

Figure 3.2 Example of a headnote on cited cases from *R v Paquette*, 1990 CanLII 37 (SCC), [1990] 2 SCR 1103

citation type (Figure 3.2). Using regular expressions, a form of natural language processing that looks for patterns in full text, we extracted and mapped citation types to the cited cases. On that basis, we were able to eliminate all instances of negative treatment, that is, of a citation distinguishing or overruling a precedent.[31] This left us with 9,295 cross-references.

We then used the ensuing list of positive or neutral cross-citations between cases dealing with constitutional law to create a citation network.[32] Network measures, rather than raw counts, were used to identify the most important nodes within a network. Following Fowler and Jeon, we relied on a weighted indegree measure known as "authority score" to measure the importance of a precedent. The authority scores of a case are proportional to the outward relevance of the cases that cite it.[33] The reasoning is that cases tend to be more important (i.e. have higher authority scores) when they are cited by decisions that in turn attract many citations. Scores are rescaled and the cases are ranked, producing an authority score of 1 for the highest-ranking case and lower percentile ranks for all other cases, depending on their authority within the network.

Following Fowler and Jeon, we investigated such authority scores over time to gain insights into how the role of a precedent evolves over the years. To this end, we partitioned the network from 1985 onwards incrementally, adding year to year until we reach 2021, such that each partition included all cases and citations up until that time, and we calculated authority scores for each decision for each partition. Plotting this

---

31 Specifically, we only included citations that were described as "Applied", "Considered", "Followed", "Referred", "Explained", "Cited", or "Adopted".

32 This analysis was done in the programming language R and using the package igraph. Input is a link list of all citing and cited cases.

33 Fowler et al., *supra* note 26 at 330; Fowler and Jeon, *supra* note 24 at 17, 20.

data allows researchers to visualize "how the importance of each decision changes through time, and perhaps more importantly, the *speed* at which precedents become *legally influential*".[34]

To illustrate the results from this operation and to highlight how these authority scores over time can differ meaningfully from raw citation counts, Figure 3.3 compares two landmark constitutional cases. *R v Collins* received as many citations within the constitutional network (in absolute numbers) as *BC Motor*.[35] However, its authority scores are only half those of *BC Motor*. *Collins*'s place within the network is therefore more peripheral, while *BC Motor*'s is more central. As noted below, *Collins*'s lower authority scores can be explained by that fact that it resolves a question bound to a specific area of law, namely search and seizure cases and the exclusion of evidence in criminal matters due to a Charter violation.

3.5 Precedential Archetypes

Network analysis enables researchers to identify the place of each precedent in the citation network and to quantify its importance within the network. It thus tells us thousands of stories about the rise and fall of individual precedents. In this chapter, we provide a glimpse of the life of precedent within the network of constitutional Supreme Court decisions by focusing on four case archetypes. Each archetype is associated with distinct patterns with varying authority scores: (1) the eternal star, (2) the forgotten pioneer, (3) the central focal point, and (4) the niche anchor. Figure 3.4 presents landmark cases that exemplify these archetypes and uses graphs to depict their rise and fall in authority scores. These cases were inductively chosen for their varying trajectories after inspecting the authority score patterns of the 20 highest-ranking cases.

3.5.1 The Eternal Star[36]

Based on authority scores, the most important case in the constitutional network is *R v Oakes*.[37] In that seminal case, the Supreme Court

---

34 Fowler and Jeon, *supra* note 24 at 25. Emphasis in original.
35 *R v Collins*, [1987] 1 SCR 265, 38 DLR (4th) 508; *Re BC Motor Vehicle Act*, [1985] 2 SCR 486, 24 DLR (4th) 536 [*BC Motor*]. As of 2021, *R v Collins* had been cited by 125 constitutional cases, and *Re BC Motor Vehicle Act* by 122.
36 We should not use the term "eternal" too literally: of course, there may come a time when the *Oakes* test is displaced and this precedent is no longer cited with the same frequency, but such a development is difficult to envision under the current state of the law.
37 *R v Oakes*, [1986] 1 SCR 103, 26 DLR (4th) 200.

Authority scores over time for *Re BC Motor Vehicle Act* and *R v Collins*

Cumulative citations for *Re BC Motor Vehicle Act* and *R v Collins*

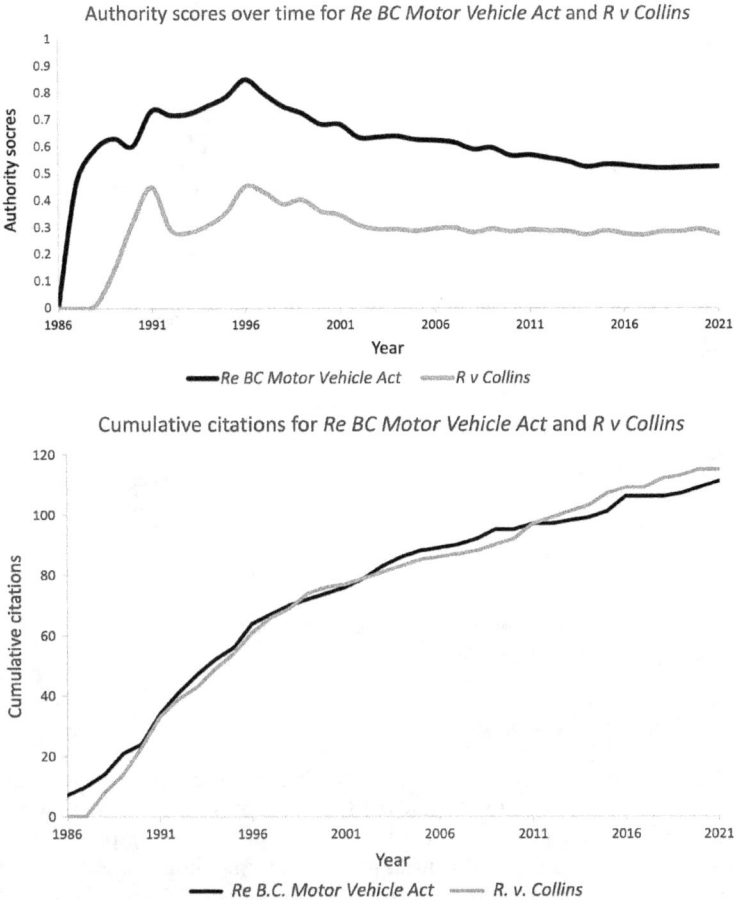

Figure 3.3 Upper panel: Line graph showing authority scores over time for *Re BC Motor Vehicle Act* and *R v Collins*. Lower panel: Line graph showing cumulative citation counts over time for *Re BC Motor Vehicle Act* and *R v Collins*

established the test for justifying infringements of Charter rights under section 1. It is bound to be cited almost every time the Court assesses whether an alleged or confirmed infringement of the Charter is demonstrably justified in a free and democratic society. Within the constitutional network, *R v Oakes* attained an authority score of 1 in 1991 – merely five years after its issuance – and has maintained its position since. It is

Authority scores over time for select constitutional cases

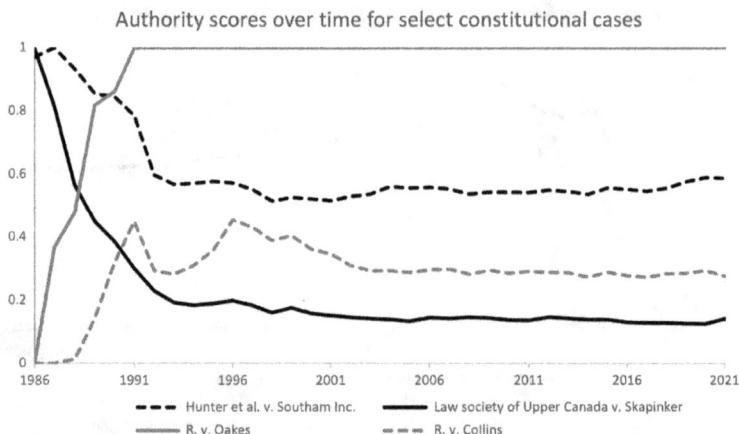

Figure 3.4 Line graph showing authority scores over time for select constitutional
cases

relatively unique in that throughout its over three decade-long presence
within the network, its authority score has never experienced a downturn.
This reflects *R v Oakes*'s consistent relevance and central role within the
Supreme Court's jurisprudence.

3.5.2 *The Displaced Pioneer*

When cases involving the newly adopted Charter started making their way
to the Supreme Court in the mid-1980s, the Court had to grapple with
novel issues, which inevitably led to it setting path-breaking precedents.
While some have remained central to our understanding of the Charter,
others have faded into the background. *Law society of Upper Canada v
Skapinker*, which was among the first Supreme Court decisions concerning the Charter,[38] represents a vivid example of such a displaced pioneer.

The case required the Court to consider whether the requirement of
holding Canadian citizenship or being a British subject for membership in
the Ontario bar contravened section 6 of the Charter. More specifically,
the Court had to determine whether paragraph 6(2)(b) of the Charter

---

38 As Justice Estey, speaking for the Court, explicitly notes near the end of the judgment,
   "[t]he originating notice which started these proceedings was one of the first under the
   Charter": *Law society of Upper Canada v Skapinker*, [1984] 1 SCR 357 at 383–384, 9
   DLR (4th) 161 [*Skapinker*].

enshrined a right to work separate from interprovincial mobility rights. This involved discussing the unique status of the Charter as a part of the Canadian Constitution and required an examination of the role of cross-headings in constitutional interpretation. Because of its role in establishing general principles of statutory interpretation that were particularly relevant in the Charter context, *Skapinker* was cited nearly every year until the turn of the century, when it continued to be cited every few years, though there was a nearly decade-long dry spell between 2011 and 2020 – a sign of the case's diminishing importance.

Interestingly, several of the cases that cited *Skapinker* early on were profoundly influential cases – strong authorities themselves – such as *Singh v Minister of Employment and Immigration*,[39] *R v Big M Drug Mart Ltd*,[40] *R v Therens*,[41] *Re BC Motor Vehicle Act*, and *R v Oakes*. These connections within the constitutional network contributed to *Skapinker*'s high authority scores in its early years, but may also help explain its seemingly exponential decline: *Skapinker* was overtaken by these even more important and widely applicable cases, such that its relative importance decreased until it reached a relatively steady state around 2005. For example, *Skapinker* was often referred to only indirectly, through the inclusion of a well-known quote from *Big M* describing and mandating the purposive approach to Charter interpretation.[42] The *Big M* quote itself points to *Skapinker* as a case that illustrates the importance of placing the Charter right at issue "in its proper linguistic, philosophic and historical context" in order to avoid "overshoot[ing] the actual purpose of the right or freedom in question" and instead to "recall that the Charter was not enacted in a vacuum".[43] Later cases tend to only refer to *Big M* for a statement of the general principle without mentioning *Skapinker*. Thus, *Skapinker*'s authority scores waned, but despite a lack of citations for almost a decade, its authority did not decline to 0, which illustrates how network-aware measures capture its continued, implied role in the chain novel of Canada's constitutional jurisprudence.

Normatively, *Skapinker* illustrates a disadvantage that can be associated with coming first: as a pioneer grappling with the constitutional status of the Charter and with the appropriate approach to interpreting such a document, it was later displaced by what became settled Charter precedent. Its pioneering role was largely forgotten as the law evolved.

---

39 [1985] 1 SCR 177, 17 DLR (4th) 422.
40 [1985] 1 SCR 295, 18 DLR (4th) 321 [*Big M*].
41 [1985] 1 SCR 613, 18 DLR (4th) 655.
42 See for example *Divito v Canada (Public Safety and Emergency Preparedness)*, 2013 SCC 47 at para. 19.
43 *Big M*, *supra* note 40 at 344.

3.5.3 The Central Focal Point

High authority scores indicate that a case is decidedly central within a network, suggesting profound legal relevance. *Hunter v Southam*[44] has exhibited such high authority scores throughout most of its existence. It deals with a cross-cutting constitutional issue, namely the purposive approach to constitutional interpretation, which projects it to the very centre of the network.

In *Hunter v Southam*, the Court expounded on the protection against unreasonable search and seizure provided by section 8 of the Charter, when tasked with determining whether the search and seizure powers granted by the *Combines Investigation Act* were inconsistent with that provision and thus unconstitutional. It is in this context that the Court developed the purposive approach to constitutional interpretation; indeed, *Hunter v Southam* has repeatedly been cited to describe this approach and to point to its origins. The decision's relevance beyond the application of section 8 helps explain why it has been consistently cited over the years, usually several times within a year. Nevertheless, *Hunter v Southam*'s authority scores did suffer a modest fall in the first fifteen years following its issuance, suggesting that this case may have experienced a mild version of the pioneer effect described above: *Hunter v Southam* was slightly displaced by – or, at least, had to compete with – other landmark cases such as *Big M* and *BC Motor Vehicle Act* that expanded on the purposive approach to interpretation.

3.5.4 The Niche Anchor

If some cases are central focal points for large segments of the network, others dominate the periphery. This is often true of decisions settling niche questions, as exemplified by *R v Collins*. In that case, in addition to dealing with the protection against unreasonable search and seizure guaranteed under section 8, the Supreme Court laid out for the first time a test for determining the admissibility of evidence in the presence of a Charter violation, namely whether admitting the evidence would bring the administration of justice into disrepute. While that test was eventually reformulated in *R v Grant*[45] in 2009, *R v Collins* has nonetheless been cited by the SCC nearly every year, often at least twice a year, since it was issued in 1987.

This case's authority score graph showcases an initial "bump" within the first five years after it was rendered. This "bump" in 1991 might be

---

44 *Hunter et al. v Southam Inc*, [1984] 2 SCR 145, 11 DLR (4th) 641 [*Hunter v Southam*].
45 2009 SCC 32; see paras 67–86.

explained by the fact there were numerous cases citing *R v Collins* in both 1989 and 1990. Several early cases citing *R v Collins* merely applied its principles; these included cases that may not have made their way up to the SCC if it were not for the fact that the law was unsettled before the decision in *R v Collins* was issued. Then, the case continued to receive several citations per year until 1999, contributing to high authority scores over that period. A subsequent slowing down of the citation rate, accompanied by a modest decrease in authority scores, may have resulted from the fact that, as this area of law became more settled, fewer cases made their way to the Supreme Court.

The pattern of a "niche anchor" thus suggests that a case *settled* a question of law – at least for some time – and has been repeatedly referenced for that reason. The normative stability thus created is demonstrated by near constant authority scores. At the same time, *R v Collins's* authority scores do not rival those of *Hunter v Southam* or *BC Motor* due to its narrower realm of relevance, but its stable pattern confirms that it is a foundational constitutional precedent, albeit in a more peripheral area.

3.6 Conclusion

In this chapter, we demonstrated that network analysis combined with natural language processing can quantitatively trace the rise and fall of precedent in ways that are normatively more aligned with how legal scholars think about precedent. The resulting metrics are thus superior to raw citation counts and to an indiscriminate analysis of citations that does not differentiate between citation types. We also presented a set of archetypes that illustrate different trajectories in the possible lives of precedent before the SCC. Importantly, this analysis was not meant to be comprehensive – other archetypes, including, for example, the afterlives of overruled precedents, remain to be explored. Our goal was, rather, to whet lawyers' appetites for the insights network analysis can provide.

Future research opportunities applying similar methods abound. Citation metrics can be compared to textbook accounts or legal briefs to validate or challenge the legal community's perception of leading cases. Citation networks can reveal unexpected or missing links that can help scholars understand how the chain novel of Canadian law was written or rewritten and how it branched out or grew more interconnected. Besides zooming out, scholars can also zoom in. For example, a case like *Collins* can be cited for different legal propositions. To accurately capture these nuances, citation metrics would need to link paragraphs or even sentences rather entire decisions. In short, this chapter, like much of this book, is meant to start, rather than wrap up, a research conversation.

Part 2

Cleavages on the Court

4 Navigating Judicial Disagreement

Carissima Mathen, Keenan MacNeal, Stephen Bindman, and Kelley Humber[1]

4.1 Introduction

Judicial disagreement is powerful. It suggests roads not taken and other possible legal worlds. It brings to the fore a fundamental and, sometimes, unsettling contingency about law.

On a high court, disagreement can appear problematic.[2] Because of the assumption that consensus equates with correctness, it may suggest a failure to "get it right". Frequent or predictable disagreement may damage a court's legitimacy.[3] Yet, it can also have positive aspects: articulating key legal rules and principles,[4] providing counter-narratives to orthodoxy,[5] laying the foundation for future development of law,[6] and providing necessary outlets for frustration.

Disagreement within an institution like the Supreme Court of Canada is inevitable and can be valuable. At the same time, it is not cost-free. Persistent patterns of disagreement, whether on the part of a single judge or several joining together, could suggest that the Court is fractured. That, in turn, could weaken the Court in the eyes of both the legal community and broader society.

In this chapter, we apply data science techniques to judicial disagreement. We apply an expanded understanding of "judicial disagreement"

---

1 Carissima Mathen is Full Professor, Stephen Bindman is Visiting Professor, and Keenan MacNeal and Kelley Humber are JD graduates of the Common Law Section, University of Ottawa Faculty of Law.
2 Emmett Macfarlane, "Consensus and Unanimity at the Supreme Court of Canada" (2010) 52 SCLR (2d) 379 at 384.
3 For an argument that dissenting opinions are not necessarily detrimental to authority, see Carissima Mathen, "Dissent and Judicial Authority in *Charter* Cases" (2003) 52 UNBLJ 321.
4 *R v Cinous*, 2002 SCC 29, [2002] 2 SCR 3.
5 See the judgment of Wilson J. in *R v Bernard* discussed *infra* note 36 and surrounding text.
6 Claire L'Heureux-Dubé, "The Dissenting Opinion: Voice of the Future?" (2000) 38 Osgoode Hall LJ 495; Anita S. Krishnakumar, "On the Evolution of the Canonical Dissent" (2000) 52 Rutgers LR 781; Richard A. Primus, "Canon, AntiCanon, and Judicial Dissent" (1998) 48 Duke LJ 243.

DOI: 10.4324/9781003279112-7

that, we think, helps explain the workings of an apex court like the Supreme Court of Canada. In its early years, the Court focused almost exclusively on adjudicating disputes. Since 1975, when it gained greater control over its docket,[7] that role has expanded to include expounding legal principle, identifying doctrine, and articulating constitutional norms. Such tasks require sensitive and nuanced judgments about which reasonable people can differ.

Judicial disagreement can take different forms. A judge may disagree with the result of a case (i.e. which party prevails).[8] Or a judge may agree with the result, but through a route that differs from that of other judges reaching the same outcome. The first kind of disagreement is commonly called a "dissent", while the second is called a "concurrence".

This chapter examines rates of dissent and concurrence over time, including comparisons with rates of unanimous decisions. It investigates any correlation between dissents and the sitting Chief Justice; and it looks at those who we call "High-Flyers" – jurists especially likely to disagree with their colleagues.

The discussion below reflects three principal findings.

First, we observed two distinct "eras" of fracturing. The first occurs from approximately 1986 to 1997, while the second occurs post-2015. The higher disagreement rate in the earlier era was concurrence-driven, that is, it was less related to the *outcome* of the case than to the *reasoning* leading to that outcome. The higher rate in the later era was dissent-driven.

Second, higher rates of disagreement do not appear to be driven by the overall tenure of the various Chief Justices.

Third, the concurrence-driven disagreement of the earlier era was a "whole-Court" phenomenon, meaning that all the Court's judges regularly penned concurrences while the dissent-driven disagreement of the later era is traced to a much smaller group of frequently dissenting judges.

---

7   In 1975, Parliament ended appeals as of right in civil cases, which gave the Court more control over its docket so it could focus on questions of public importance (*Supreme Court Act*, SC 1974-75-76, c 18). See also *R v Henry*, 2005 SCC 76, [2005] 3 SCR 609, at para. 53.

8   The Supreme Court also hears references, a special jurisdiction to provide "advice" in response to questions formulated by Cabinet. Because references do not involve a live case, they do not produce actual judgments. But they have been extremely important to the Court's jurisprudence. Our dataset therefore includes them. See *Supreme Court Act*, RSC, 1985, c S-26 s 53.

4.2 Approach

Using the dataset described in the introductory chapter, regular expressions were used to extract additional information, including judges present, origin of appeal, authorship, and types of disagreement.[9]

After dividing the text of each case into its constituent opinions, we tagged each opinion as a "majority", "dissent", or "concurrence".[10] Dissents were tagged based on the Court's own explicit language, either at the top of the header ("Dissenting Reasons: …"), when the opinion is introduced ("The reasons of Wagner CJ and Brown J were delivered by Brown J (dissenting)"), or in the case footer ("Appeal dismissed, Wagner CJ and Brown J dissenting"). An opinion was tagged as a majority if (1) it was the only opinion in the case; (2) it was the only non-dissenting opinion in the case; or (3) more than half of the judges who sat on the case joined the opinion. Any opinion not tagged as either a dissent or a majority was tagged as a concurrence. In total, the dataset includes 3,912 majority opinions, 1,222 dissenting opinions, and 1,262 concurring opinions. Note that under this definition of "majority", a given case may have no majority opinion (as opposed to a majority result).[11]

Some of the charts below measure disagreement by looking at categories of cases, while others focus on how individual judges participate in cases. "Case Dissent Rate" describes the proportion of cases in which one or more judges registered a dissent. Case Dissent Rate is used to show trends over time. "Judge Dissent Rate", which describes the proportion of judges who dissented across a group of cases, is used for analyses that display results by judge.[12] These different measures allow us to examine disagreement on the Court both as a whole and among its judges.

4.3 The Fractured Court

Sometimes, disagreement about a case's legal reasoning can be more significant than disagreement over its ultimate result. One example of this would be that, while agreeing on the relevant legal framework, judges

---

9 Data analysis was conducted in the coding language "R" with heavy use of open-source libraries, in particular, quanteda, stringr, and dplyr.

10 The dataset includes dissents issued from the bench.

11 For example, if a nine-judge panel agrees on the outcome of a case but split four to three to two, our scheme would classify the case as having three concurrences and no majority opinion.

12 Example: a dataset contains one case in which five judges sat and two joined a dissent. The Case Dissent Rate is 100%, because 1/1 cases in the dataset contained one or more dissents. The Judge Dissent Rate is 40%, because 2/5 judges in the dataset dissented. A dataset with one case in which eight judges joined the majority and one judge dissented would have a case dissent rate of 100% and a judge dissent rate of ~11%.

disagree over how to apply it. Another would be that judges divide over how much deference to grant a lower court's findings. These sorts of disagreement will not tend to affect the precedential value of the case. Disagreement over legal reasoning, by contrast, can deeply affect whether a case has precedential value. Below, we briefly discuss some decisions that show the significance of disagreement over legal reasoning.

First, in the famous *Morgentaler* case, a majority of the Court struck down Canada's criminal abortion law as inconsistent with section 7 of the Charter.[13] But the judges in the majority did not agree on *how* the law violated section 7. Some found that, by creating obstacles to women obtaining medically required treatment, the offence violated their security of the person. Others focused on the law's infringement of personal liberty. A replacement criminal provision was never enacted. But the fractured nature of the majority has contributed to continued confusion over the case's governing principles.[14]

The second example features concurring opinions that obscure guidance about important collateral issues. In *Mikisew Cree*,[15] a First Nation objected to certain environmental legislation. The Mikisew Cree sought a declaration that federal executive actors had breached a "duty to consult" them when those actors developed the bill that Parliament ultimately passed.

The Supreme Court unanimously found that the lower court lacked the jurisdiction to grant the declaration. It also held, seven to two, that the duty to consult did not apply in the manner suggested by the Mikisew Cree, but the seven judges in the majority did not agree on the implications of that holding. Some favoured a strict, bright-line rule against any judicial remedy,[18] while others thought that it might be possible to grant other forms of relief.[17] One of the judges in the former group went so far as to castigate his other colleagues for throwing the law into "significant uncertainty".[16]

Finally, concurring opinions in one case can end up informing a majority decision in another. In *R v Bernard*, the Court considered whether self-induced intoxication might create reasonable doubt about a defendant's ability to form the intent to commit a crime.[17] A five-to-two

---

13   *R v Morgentaler*, [1988] 1 SCR 30. Section 7 of the Charter guarantees everyone "life, liberty and security of the person", subject only to deprivations that accord with "the principles of fundamental justice".

14   Mark Gollum, "Why Canada's Roe v. Wade Didn't Enshrine Abortion as a Right" *CBC News* May 4, 2022: https://www.cbc.ca/news/canada/abortion-rights-canada-morgentaler-court-1.6439612.

15   *Mikisew Cree First Nation v Canada (Governor General in Council)*, 2018 SCC 40.

16   Ibid., per Brown J. at para. 104.

17   *R v Bernard*, [1988] 2 SCR 833.

majority ruled that the case lacked sufficient evidence of the effects of alleged intoxication on Bernard himself. It diverged on the more fundamental question of whether intoxication could ever "negate" intent. Justice Bertha Wilson, concurring, argued that the law should allow for such a possibility. Six years later, a new majority of the Court took up Wilson J.'s analysis.[18] That majority held that the *Charter of Rights* forbids the conviction of a person who at the time of the alleged offence was so extremely intoxicated as to be blacked out.[19]

These examples show why concurring opinions are an important feature of Supreme Court disagreement. They illuminate ways in which a Court may be fractured such that its ability to render clear authoritative guidance on the law is diminished.

The next several charts show a number of ways to represent disagreement on the Supreme Court between 1975 and 2021. We begin with Figure 4.1, which shows the percentage of cases each year in which the Court was unanimous. It shows that unanimity was most common in the early 1980s, decreased from the late 1980s to mid-1990s, was relatively stable during the early 2000s, became highly variable in the late 2000s and early 2010s, and has decreased since 2015.

These trends are clearer in Figure 4.2, which shows the proportion of the Court's written output stemming from unanimous judgments. This number can be thought of as the likelihood that a word chosen at random from any case is part of a unanimous judgment. Justices have a finite time to write. The proportion of text in unanimous judgments in a year can function as a proxy for the intensity of disagreement during that year. If the judges spend their limited time crafting lengthy unanimous judgments, that may indicate that the disagreements between the judges are shallower or more transient than if the judges are spending their time writing lengthy opinions in fractured cases.

Applying this text-based metric to the Court's recent history, Figure 4.2 shows two major eras of fracturing. These periods are marked by the proportion of text from unanimous judgments reaching sustained, multi-year lows. The first era occurred from approximately 1986 to 1997. The second, which started in 2015, is ongoing at the time of writing. Although the portion of text from unanimous judgments dropped substantially in 2007 and 2009, this was not sustained across multiple years, as in the two periods we have identified.

Figure 4.3 shows the rate at which judges joined dissenting opinions in each year for which we have data. We chose to investigate disagreement using judge-based metrics rather than case-based metrics because

18 *R v Daviault*, [1994] 3 SCR 63.
19 That analysis was confirmed, unanimously, in *R v Brown*, 2022 SCC 18.

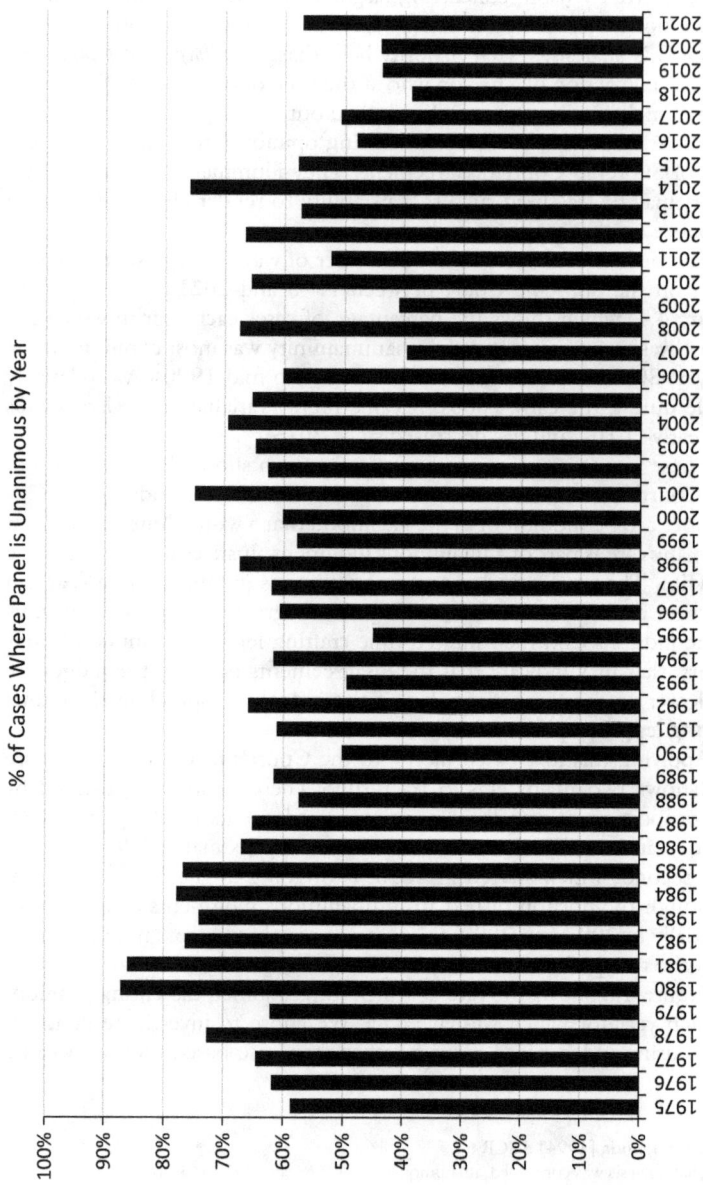

Figure 4.1 Percent of cases where panel is unanimous by year.

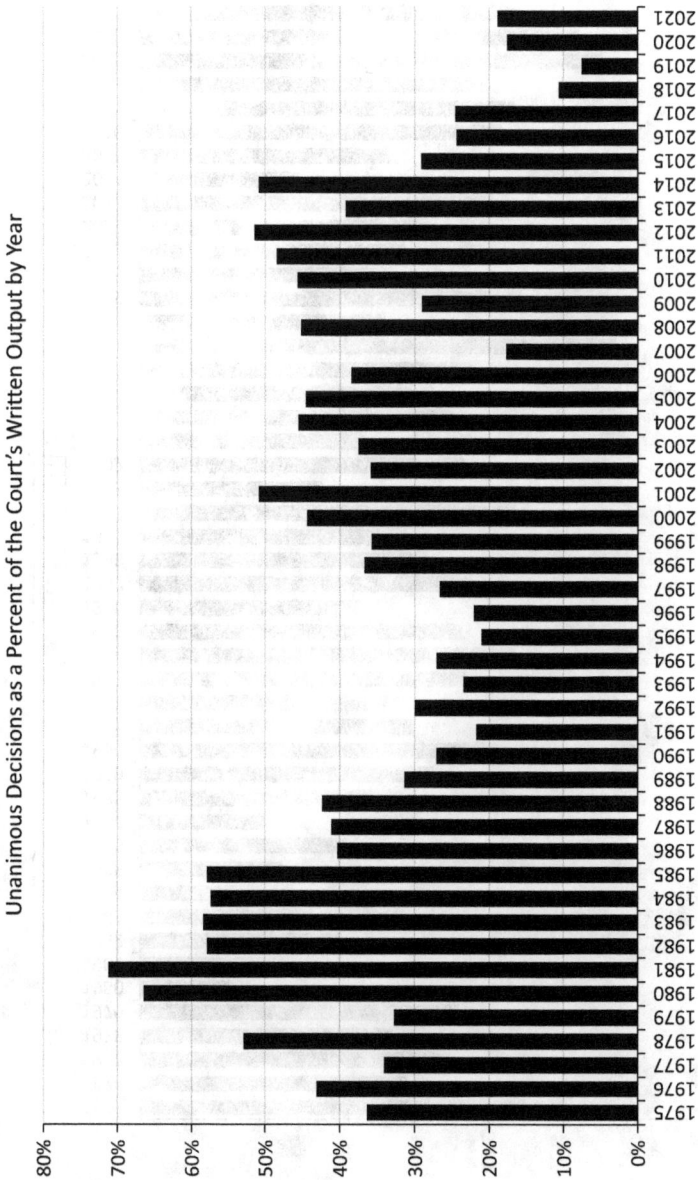

Figure 4.2 Unanimous decisions as a percent of the court's written output by year.

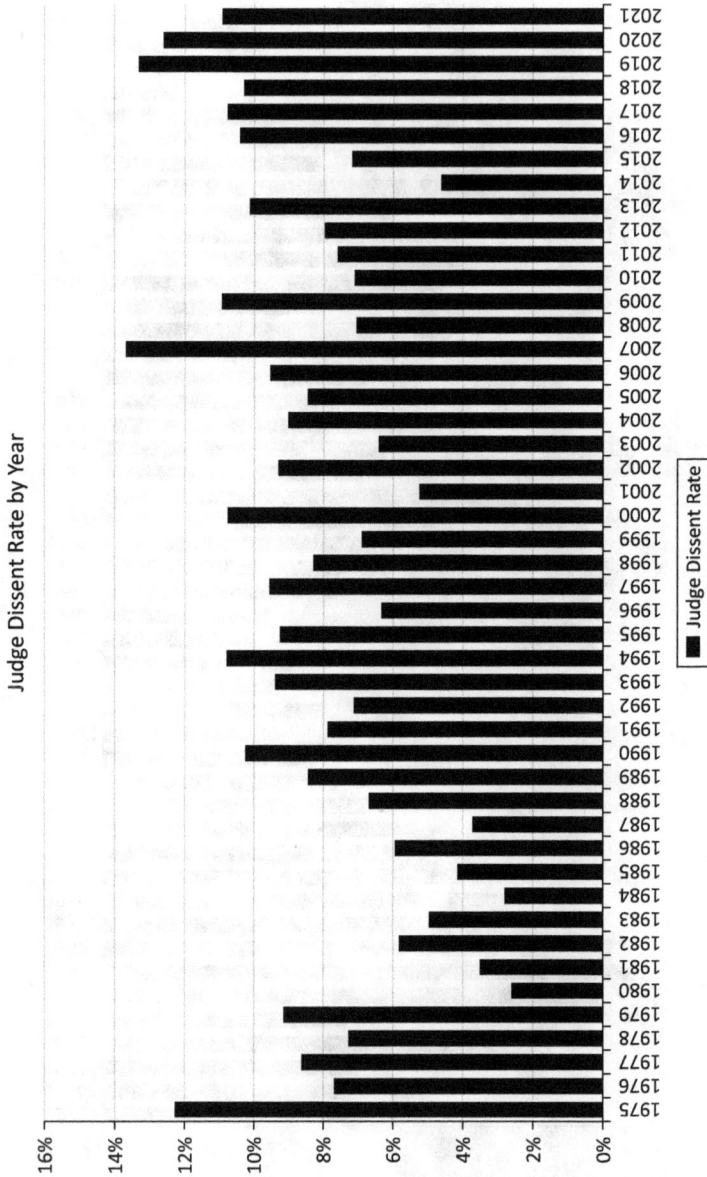

Figure 4.3 Judge dissent rate by year

the former provides a fuller account of the scale of disagreement between the judges – in our view, there is less disagreement in a hypothetical year in which every case is divided eight to one than one where every case is decided five to four. The percentage figures can be understood as the average rate at which, in any given case, a judge joined a dissent.[20] Representing rates of dissent "by judge", rather than "by case", reduces the impact of individual judges that joined dissents or concurrences at anomalously high rates.[21]

Figure 4.3 provides strong evidence that the more recent decrease in unanimity has been driven by increases in the judge *dissent* rate. From 1975 to 2015, dissent rates exceeded 10% in ten separate years. From 2016 to 2021, the rate exceeded 10% every single year. This supports present-day impressions that the current Court is more fractured than in the recent past.[22]

If the earlier era of fracturing is not well explained by judge *dissent* rate, then it must relate to the rate at which judges joined *concurring opinions*. This premise is confirmed by Figure 4.4, which shows the judge concurrence rate by year. The increase is unmistakable: judges joined concurrences most frequently in the late 1980s and early 1990s, with a peak in 1990. Across our whole dataset, the judge concurrence rate exceeded 10% in only eight years, all between 1986 and 1996.

The earlier, concurrence-driven nature of the first era of fracturing can also be seen by examining cases without a majority opinion. High rates of concurrence are correlated with cases lacking majority opinions because a case with no majority opinion will necessarily have two or more concurrences instead.[23]

Figure 4.5 shows the number of cases per year with no majority opinion. These are represented as absolute values, which means that the bars do not account for the varying number of cases heard by the Court each year.[24] The preponderance of cases with no majority opinion occurred in the late 1980s and early 1990s, matching the observed increase in judge

---

20 For example, in 2021, the judge dissent rate was 10.5%. That means that for any given case in 2021, each individual judge sitting on that case had a 10.5% likelihood of joining a dissent.

21 See note 14 for additional explanation.

22 Sean Fine, "Canada's Supreme Court Is Off-Balance as 'Large and Liberal' Consensus on the Charter Falls Apart" *The Globe and Mail* January 15, 2022: https://www.theglobeandmail.com/canada/article-canadas-supreme-court-is-off-balance-as-large-and-liberal-consensus-on/.

23 In *R v. Wholesale Travel Group*, [1991] 3 S.C.R. 154, the defendant argued, successfully, that the competition law offence infringed the presumption of innocence. The five-judge majority split three to two on why that was the case. In our data, both the three-judge opinion and the two-judge opinion would be classified as concurring opinions.

24 The labels above each bar indicate the total number of cases the Court heard in the year.

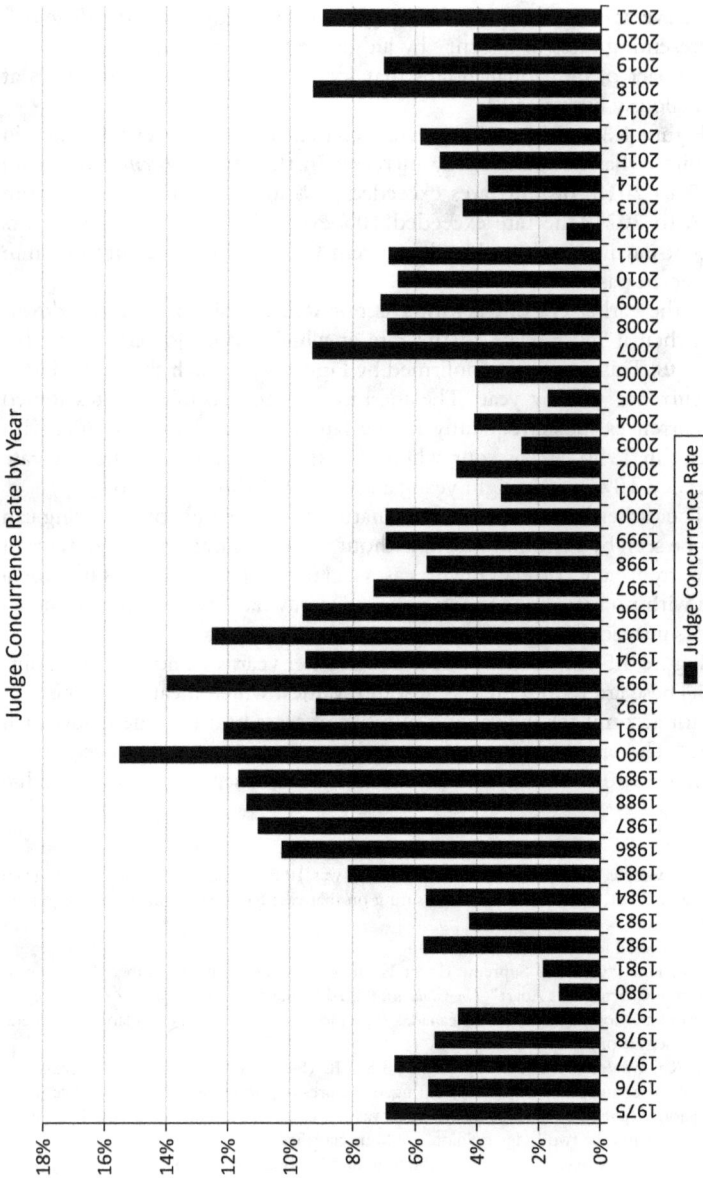

Figure 4.4 Judge concurrence rate by year

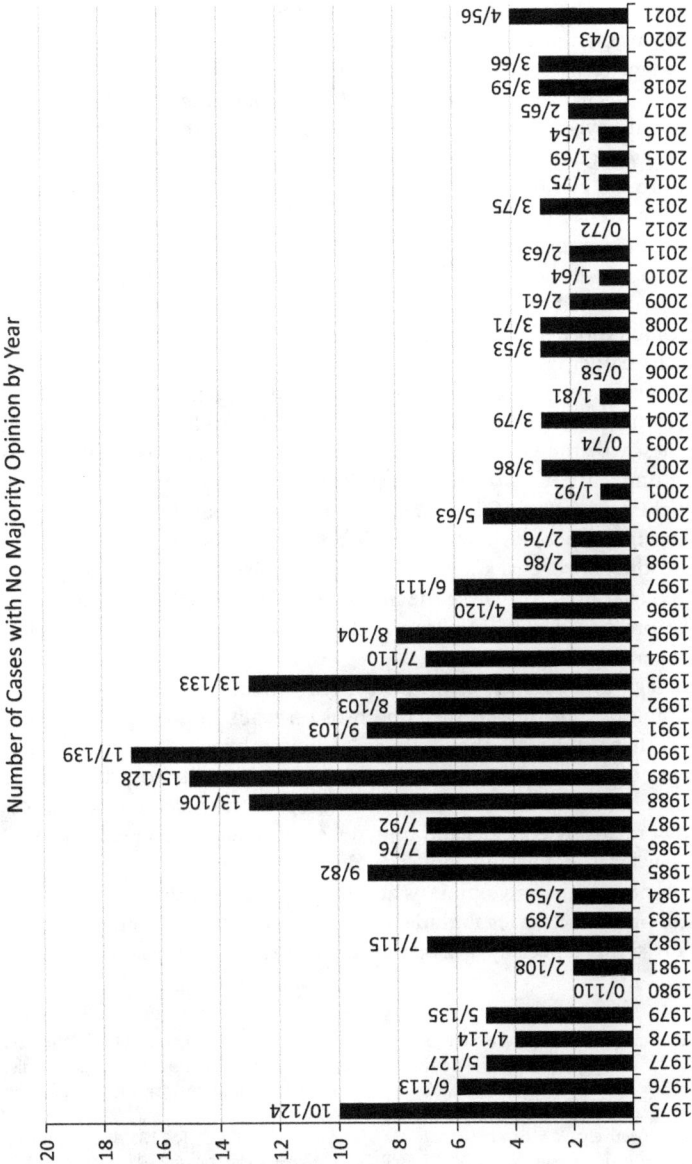

Figure 4.5 Number of cases with no majority opinion by year

concurrence rate. The number of cases with no majority opinion also peaked in 1990, the same year that the overall judge concurrence rate peaked.

Figure 4.6 shows the three-year moving average of the judge dissent rate and judge concurrence rate data represented in Figures 4.3 and 4.4. Moving averages are a technique that makes it easier to observe and compare longer-term trends by "smoothing" out how the data appears in data visualizations like charts and graphs.[25] In this chart, the dotted line shows the moving average of judge dissent rates, and the solid line shows the moving average of judge concurrence rates.

Figure 4.6 clarifies the differences between the two eras of fracturing. The concurrence-driven nature of the first era can be seen in a growing rate of concurrence in the late 1980s/early 1990s period. The dissent-driven nature of the second era can be seen in the dotted line's sharp rise in the second half of the 2010s. Figure 4.6 also demonstrates that judges have joined more dissents than concurrences since the late 1990s.

In the earlier era of fracturing, the judges' disagreement was concurrence-driven, so the decrease in unanimity during this period is correlated with rates of concurrence. The concurrence-driven disagreement coincides with the years that the Court's docket began to include cases arising under the *Constitution Act, 1982*. Among other things, that Act entrenched a *Charter of Rights and Freedoms* and constitutional rights for the Aboriginal peoples of Canada. It represented a profound paradigm shift for the entire legal system. It is not surprising that the judges would disagree over how to analyse the new issues that inevitably arose.[26]

The preceding analysis helps to refine the "fractured" narrative mentioned earlier.

If a lack of unanimity stems primarily from an abundance of concurring opinions, but there is the consensus on whether an appeal succeeds or fails, that may create the illusion of a united bench. However, higher numbers of concurrences may affect the Court's ability to provide clear guidance on the state of the law. Such disagreement creates the impression of a relatively collegial and united Court, while simultaneously making it harder to define and apply the Court's precedents.

In contrast, majority opinions attended by strongly expressed dissents can still provide clear legal guidance. But high dissent rates may suggest deep divisions, especially if dissents are consistently coming from judicial

---

25 With a moving average, the data shown at each point in time is an ensemble of the data over the preceding period of time (in this case, three years). For instance, the dotted dissent line shows a value of approximately 12% in 2021. That means that the overall judge dissent rate across 2019, 2020, and 2021 was 12%.

26 See, respectively, *R v Edwards Books and Art Ltd.*, [1986] 2 SCR 713; *Andrews v Law Society of British Columbia*, [1989] 1 SCR 143; *Guerin v The Queen*, [1984] 2 SCR 335.

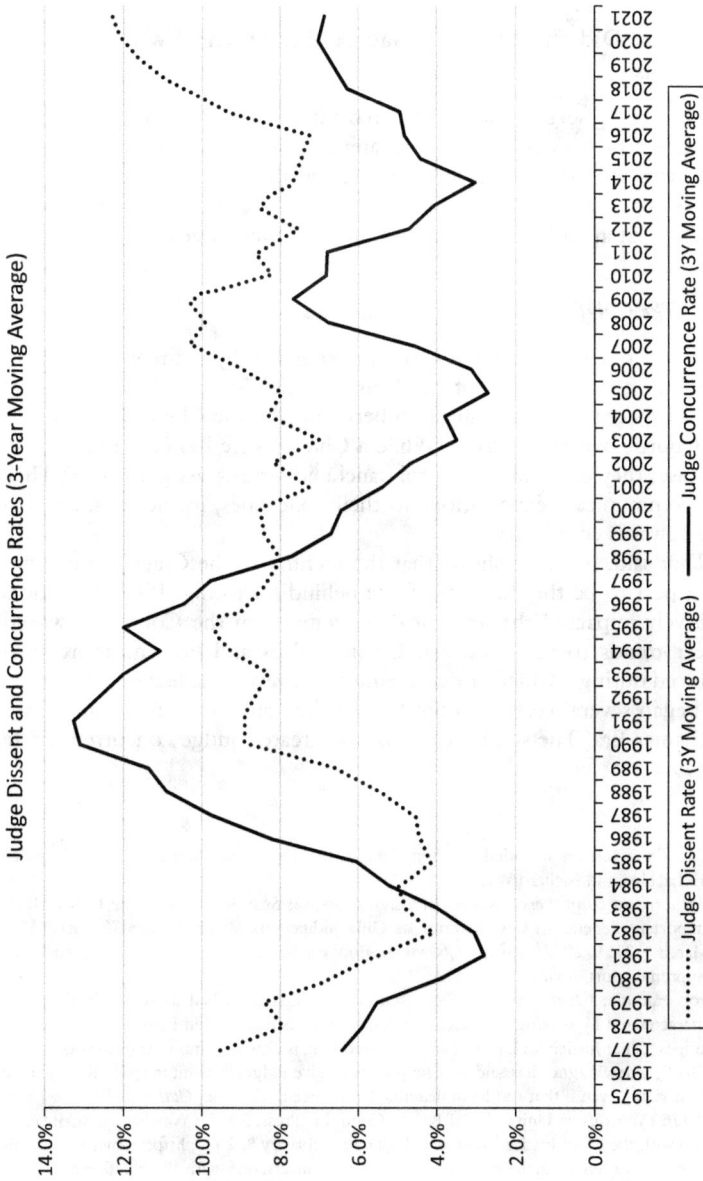

Figure 4.6 Judge dissent and concurrence rates (3-year moving average)

blocs. This may tempt Court observers to focus on the individual judges on the bench in a way that undermines the longer-term legitimacy of the Court.

4.4 Why Did the Judges Disagree during the Two Eras?

The preceding section identified two distinct eras of fracturing: an earlier one driven by concurrences, and a later one driven by dissents.

In this section, we begin to probe the thorny question of *why* the judges might have disagreed so frequently in the two eras. We do so by looking first at Chief Justices,[27] and then at other judges.

4.4.1 The Chiefs

We begin our more judge-focused investigation by examining disagreement during the tenures of the Court's Chief Justices. Intuitively, one might expect to find a connection between who the Chief Justice is, and the Court's overall cohesion. While a Chief Justice has only one vote in any case, they do tend to control panel and writing assignments.[28] They also communicate expectations to their colleagues, including their attitude towards consensus.[29]

That said, our data shows that the identity of the Chief Justice does *not* appear to be the dominant force behind fracturing. If Chief Justices decisively impacted the level of disagreement on the Court, we would expect trends to vary between Chief Justices and become more pronounced during a Chief Justice's tenure. However, the first era of fracturing began several years into the Dickson Era and continued solidly into the Lamer Era. The single year with the greatest judge concurrence rate

---

27 The Chief Justices included are Bora Laskin, Brian Dickson, Antonio Lamer, Beverley McLachlin, and Richard Wagner.

28 For a recent controversy over panel assignments, see Sean Fine, "Supreme Court Hears Important Federalism Case without Its Only Indigenous Member" *The Globe and Mail* March 21, 2023: https://www.theglobeandmail.com/canada/article-seven-judge -supreme-court-environmental-case/.

29 For example, Chief Justice Lamer's tenure has been described as relatively fractious, characterized by striking gendered divisions as well as real tension between at least some judges. Chief Justice McLachlin, who followed him, is viewed as more consensus-oriented. Chief Justice Wagner has said that he prefers to give judges maximum space to articulate their views, even if that results in dissents. Constance Backhouse, *Claire L'Heureux-Dubé: A Life* (Vancouver: University of British Columbia Press, 2017); Yves Faguy, "Conversation with the Chief Justice" *National Magazine* February 8, 2022: https://www.national-magazine.ca/en-ca/articles/people/q-a/2022/conversation-with-the-chief-justice.

was 1990 – the year that the Dickson Era transitioned to the Lamer Era. The second era of fracturing started in approximately 2015, two years before the start of the Wagner Era. While Chief Justices may play a role in shaping discourse on the Court, other underlying factors seem to be driving varying trends in disagreement.

Furthermore, the individual dissenting and concurring behaviours of Chief Justices only loosely correspond to the patterns of disagreement observed during their respective tenures. Figure 4.7 shows the dissent rate and concurrence rate for each judge in our data. Each judge is represented by a dot. Dissent rate is shown from left to right; the further to the right a dot appears, the higher the rate at which that judge dissented. Concurrence rates are shown vertically, with greater rates of concurrence placed higher on the chart. To improve readability, only selected judges are labelled. These judges include the most dissenting and most concurring justices, along with every Chief Justice.

Among the Chief Justices, Chief Justice Laskin dissented most frequently at 13%, but note that our data only includes his tenure from 1975 onward. This is in contrast to the Laskin Era, which saw some of the lowest overall rates of dissent. Chief Justices Dickson, Lamer, McLachlin, and Wagner all dissented at rates within two percentage points of the overall median of 7%, despite the wide range in overall rates of dissent during their tenures. The Chief Justices' rates of concurrence are more evenly distributed from Chief Justice Lamer's high of almost 11% and Chief Justice Wagner's low of just above 5%. Chief Justice McLachlin

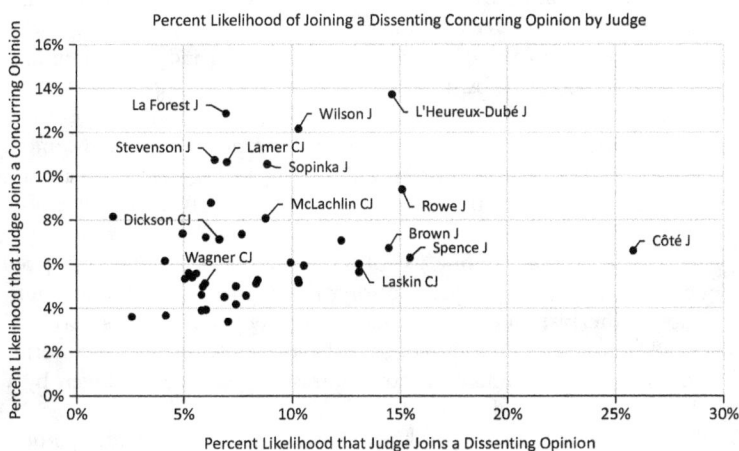

Figure 4.7 Percent likelihood of joining a dissenting of concurring opinion by judge

is the second most concurring Chief Justice, but during her tenure the Court saw a relatively smaller number of concurrences. Chief Justice Lamer is the exception; his high rate of concurrence matches the overall trend of his era.

4.4.2 *"High-Flyers"*

What about the other judges? Figure 4.7 also provides an overview of the observed range of dissent rates and concurrence rates.

Figure 4.7 shows that more than half of judges dissent between 5% and 10% of the time, and more than half concur between 4% and 8% of the time. This can be seen in the relatively tight cluster of dots in the lower left quadrant of the chart.

Looking beyond Chief Justices, the distribution of dissents and concurrences aligns well with the two eras of fracturing. We see that a group of six judges has had the highest rate of concurrence: Justices L'Heureux-Dubé, La Forest, Wilson, Stevenson, Lamer, and Sopinka. All six were on the Court during the first, concurrence-driven era of fracturing. Of the five most *dissenting* judges, three have been on the Court during the second, more recent era of fracturing: Justices Côté, Rowe, and Brown.

This pattern is to be expected. A judge who joins dissents or concurrences at an anomalously high rate will increase the overall rate at which the judges join dissents and concurrences. As an analogy, the rosters of the highest-scoring sports teams usually include some of the highest-scoring individual players.

What we did *not* necessarily expect in the two eras was a notable difference in concurrence versus dissent rates.

Figure 4.8 shows the concurrence rate for each judge in ascending order, with indicators showing each judge who heard 50 or more cases during the first era of fracturing (late 1980s to early 1990s). Judges from that first era dominate the top end of this metric. All six of the most concurring judges (see above) served during this time – and they are the only judges in our data with concurrence rates above 10%. Of the 15 most concurring judges, 12 served during this period.

This suggests that the first era of fracturing was a whole-court phenomenon. Almost all the judges during this period concurred at a rate well above the historical norm. Only two judges during this period – Justices Major and Iacobucci – concurred at or below the historical norm.

The second era of fracturing, by contrast, appears to be driven by a much small group of judges.

Figure 4.9 shows the rate of dissent for each judge in ascending order, with indicators showing which judges heard 50 or more cases during the second era of fracturing. Almost every judge in the first era of fracturing concurred at historically anomalous rates. In the second era of

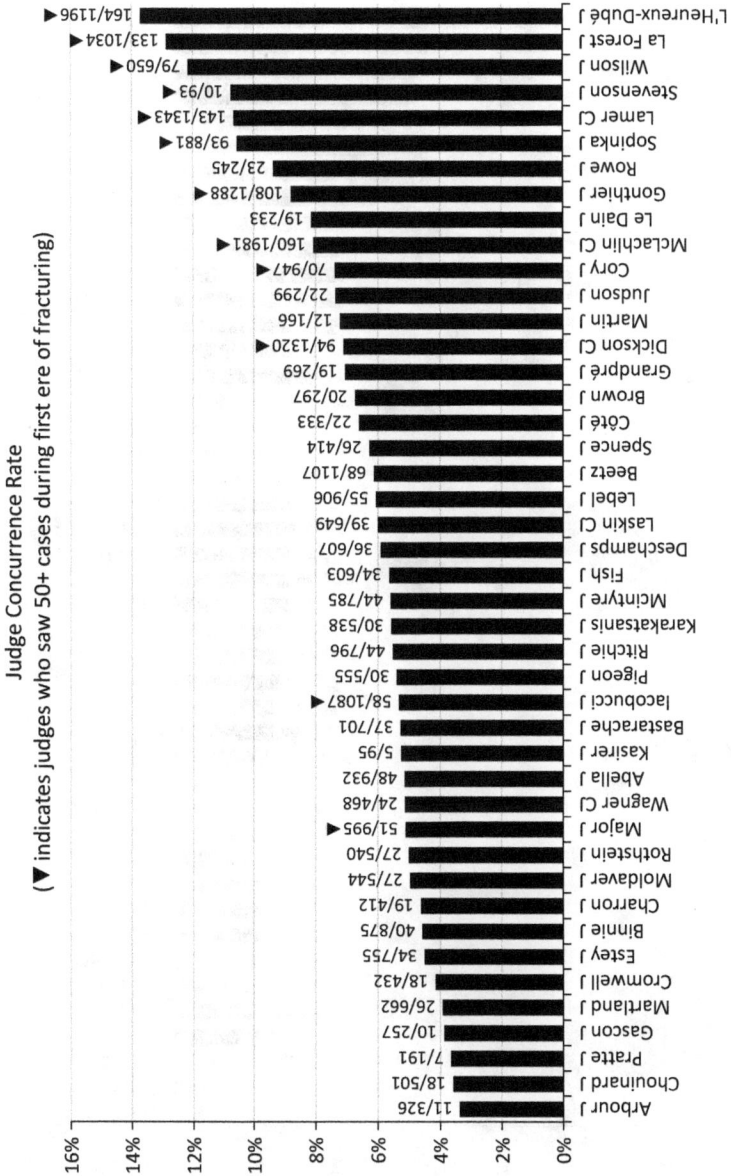

Judge Concurrence Rate

(▼ indicates judges who saw 50+ cases during first ere of fracturing)

L'Heureux-Dubé J	▼ 164/1196
La Forest J	▼ 133/1034
Wilson J	▼ 79/650
Stevenson J	▼ 10/93
Lamer CJ	▼ 143/1343
Sopinka J	▼ 93/881
Rowe J	23/245
Gonthier J	▼ 108/1288
Le Dain J	19/233
McLachlin CJ	▼ 160/1981
Cory J	▼ 70/947
Judson J	22/299
Martin J	12/166
Dickson CJ	▼ 94/1320
Grandpré J	19/269
Brown J	20/297
Côté J	22/333
Spence J	26/414
Beetz J	68/1107
Lebel J	55/906
Laskin CJ	39/649
Deschamps J	36/607
Fish J	34/603
McIntyre J	44/785
Karakatsanis J	30/538
Ritchie J	44/796
Pigeon J	30/555
Iacobucci J	▼ 58/1087
Bastarache J	37/701
Kasirer J	5/95
Abella J	48/932
Wagner CJ	24/468
Major J	▼ 51/995
Rothstein J	27/540
Moldaver J	27/544
Charron J	19/412
Binnie J	40/875
Estey J	34/755
Cromwell J	18/432
Martland J	26/662
Gascon J	10/257
Pratte J	7/191
Chouinard J	18/501
Arbour J	11/326

Figure 4.8 Judge concurrence rate (▼indicates judges who saw + cases during the first era of fracturing)

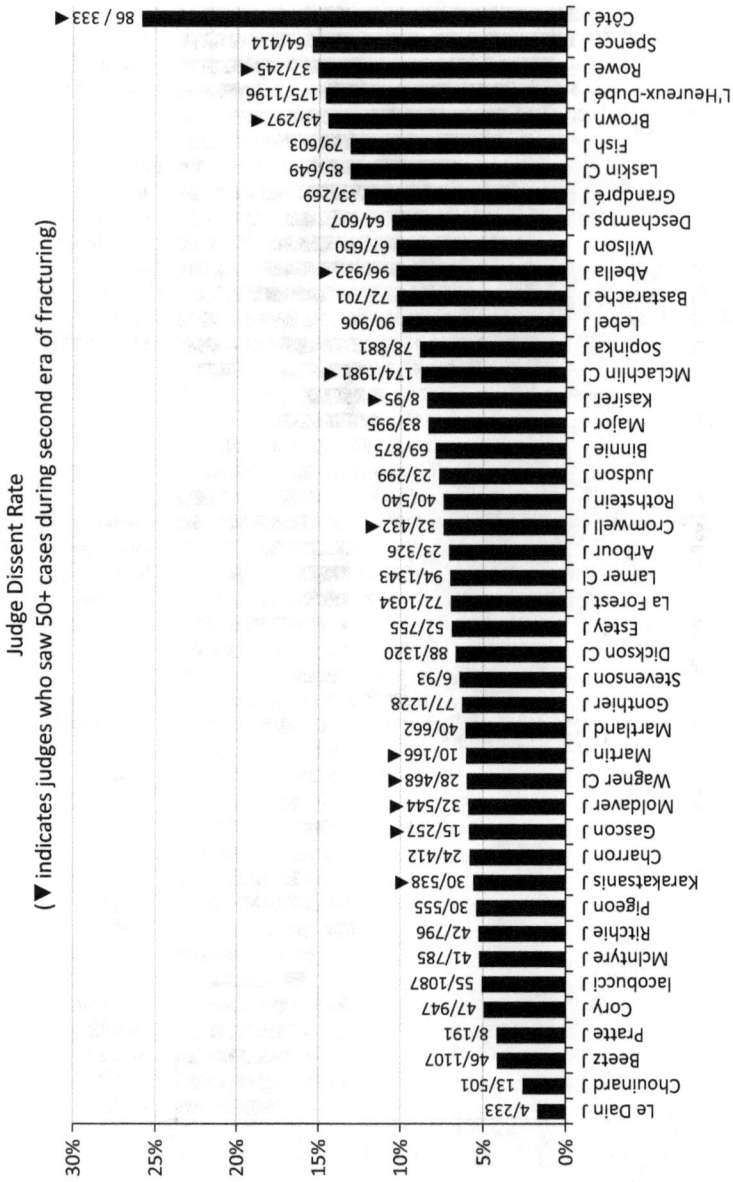

Figure 4.9 Judge dissent rate (▼indicates judges who saw + cases during the first era of fracturing during the second era of fracturing)

fracturing, the dissent rates of justices are more evenly spread out across the range. Across our whole dataset, judges dissented 8.1% of the time.[30] Justices Karakatsanis, Gascon, Moldaver, Martin, Cromwell, and Chief Justice Wagner have all dissented less frequently than this overall rate. Chief Justice McLachlin and Justices Kasirer and Abella have dissented at higher rates than average but below the "step up" that separates the top dissenters. Justices Brown, Rowe, and especially Côté are at the high end of the scale.

4.4.3 Sui Generis: *The Case of Justice Côté*

Justice Côté is a clear statistical outlier. She has dissented almost 26% of the time – far more than any other judge. Her rate is more than ten percentage points higher than the next most dissenting judge, Justice Spence. For additional perspective, ten percentage points is approximately the difference between Justice Spence's rate of dissent and Justice McIntyre's. In other words, the difference between the highest dissent rate and the second highest is the same as the difference between second highest dissent rate and the thirty-eighth highest.

Justice Côté's dissents also occur at a rate 11 percentage points higher than an earlier judge who actually has been called "The Great Dissenter": Justice L'Heureux-Dubé,[31] who is the fourth most dissenting judge in our data. Interestingly, the latter judge registered a similarly high rate of concurrences. In fact, Justice L'Heureux-Dubé's joined concurrences about 14% of the time, which makes her the single most concurring judge in our data. Most of the judges gravitate towards one form of disagreement over the other; only Justice L'Heureux-Dubé made the top-five list for both. That said, Justice Côté's dissent rate is so anomalously high that it trails behind Justice L'Heureux-Dubé's *combined* rate of dissent and concurrence by less than three percentage points.[32]

Justice Côté's dissenting behaviour is so extreme and unprecedented that she may be the person most responsible for the post-2015 era of fracturing. The three-year moving average dissent rate shown earlier in

---

30 The average of judge dissent rates was 8.3%. The median judge (Justice Arbour) dissented 7.1% of the time.

31 Marie- Claire Belleau and Rebecca Johnson, "Judging gender: difference and dissent at the Supreme Court of Canada", (2008) 15-1-2 Int J Leg Prof 60.

32 Of course, one must be careful with such comparisons. These two jurists come from different eras, saw different cases, and sat with different colleagues. It remains important to examine Justice L'Heureux-Dubé's rates compared to those of her contemporaries – work that has been covered by other scholars (ibid.; see also Constance Backhouse, *Claire L'Heureux-Dubé: A Life* (2017, UBC Press)). Nonetheless, we believe the comparison serves to illustrate the unprecedented nature of Justice Côté's dissenting.

Judge Dissent Rates Without Côté J and Without Côté, Rowe, and Brown JJ (3-Year MA)

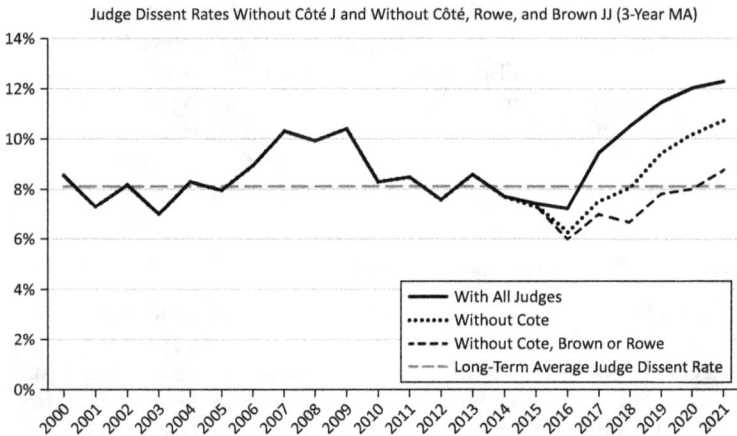

Figure 4.10 Judge dissent rates without Côté, Rowe, and Brown JJ (3-year moving average)

Figure 4.6 is reproduced in Figure 4.10 (solid line). It also shows how that metric would have looked without Justice Côté (dotted line), and without Justices Côté, Brown, or Rowe (dashed line). The horizontal, grey dashed line shows the 8.1% overall rate of dissent rate across all years and all judges in our data.

Without Justice Côté's dissents, the Court's overall rate of dissent remains near the 8.1% overall rate of dissent from 2015–2019.[33] Justice Côté's impact on the overall rate of dissent was greatest in 2018. Including her, the three-year moving average dissent rate in that year was 10.5%, the highest value recorded up to that point. Excluding Justice Côté, the dissent rate among the other judges that year was only 8%, which is *below* the long-term average rate. However, while Justice Côté appears to be responsible for much of the increased rate of dissent seen from 2015 to 2019, the dissent rate remains elevated in 2020 and especially 2021, even when calculated without her.

In 2020, the high three-year moving average dissent rate excluding Justice Côté appears to largely be driven by the dissenting habits of the Court's other two top dissenters at that time: Justices Rowe and Brown. Removing these three judges from consideration, the Court's yearly rate of dissent would have remained below the long-term average in each year

33 *Supra* note 49.

from 2015 to 2020, and only slightly above it in 2021. This means that Justices Côté, Brown, and Rowe dissented so frequently that they raise the whole Court's average dissent rate. Simply put, these three judges were solely responsible for the increased rate of dissent seen from 2015 to 2021.[34]

4.5 Conclusion and Future Work

This chapter has explored just some of the ways in which disagreement has manifested on the Supreme Court of Canada. It revealed two notable periods of fracturing since 1975: the late 1980s to the mid-1990s, and from 2015 to the time of writing. The drivers of disagreement in these two eras are different. The first is marked by high rates of concurrence while the second displays higher rates of dissent. Disagreement does not appear to correlate very closely with the position of Chief Justice. Concurrences are spread more evenly across the judges than dissents; in the second era, dissents are traceable to a small coterie of judges, with one – Justice Suzanne Côté – being responsible for an anomalously high number of dissents.

There are many other aspects of Supreme Court disagreement that could be studied using this methodology. We are intrigued by the possibilities of sentiment analysis.[35] We did not find the currently available lexicons well suited to jurisprudential analysis, but we think this area is ripe for the development of more sensitive language metrics. Another rich topic for future work is the correlation of disagreement with a case's doctrinal area (for example, criminal versus constitutional versus private law). We are interested, as well, in the extent to which there is a correlation between rates of disagreement and either the regions or courts from which cases originate. Finally, we would like to examine in greater detail how dissents or concurrences can eventually become majority opinions.

---

34 Justice Brown left the Court in 2023.
35 For a definition, see Chapter 2.

5 Bilingualism at the Supreme Court of Canada: Quantifying Citations to English, French, and Bilingual Doctrinal Sources

Terry Skolnik[1] and Keenan MacNeal[2]

5.1 Introduction

The Supreme Court of Canada (SCC) is unique in certain respects. The Court hears cases in both of Canada's official languages: English and French.[3] Yet the law does not currently require the justices to be functionally bilingual.[4] Instead, the justices can receive simultaneous translations through an interpreter.[5] Governmental policy currently dictates whether functional bilingualism is necessary for a new Supreme Court of Canada justice.[6] Throughout the Court's history, some of its justices were unilingual Anglophones when they were appointed.[7]

1 Associate Professor, University of Ottawa, Faculty of Law. Co-director of the uOttawa Public Law Centre.
2 Juris doctor (JR) candidate, University of Ottawa, Faculty of Law. We thank Amy Salazyn, Anna Maria Konewka, Carissima Mathen, Jeremy Opolsky, Michael Pal, Stephen Bindman, Vanessa MacDonnell, and Wolfgang Alschner for comments on prior drafts. We also thank Lilian Potvin and Alexandre Faubert Charlebois for their valuable research assistance. All mistakes are my own.
3 *Official Languages Act*, RSC 1985, c 31 (4th Supp), ss 14–16.
4 Jean-Christophe Bédard-Rubin and Tiago Rubin, "The Elusive Quest for French on the Bench: Bilingualism Scores for Canadian Supreme Court Justices, 1985–2013" (2022) 37:2 Can J L and Soc'y 249 at 250.
5 Jean-Christophe Bedard-Rubin and Tiago Rubin, "Assessing the Impact of Unilingualism at the Supreme Court of Canada: Panel Composition, Assertiveness, Caseload, and Deference" (2018) 55:3 Osgoode Hall LJ 713 at 720–721.
6 Alexandrea Nasager, "The Supreme Court, Functional Bilingualism, and the Indigenous Candidate: Reconciling the Bench" (2020) 57:3 Alta L Rev 797 at 798.
7 Jean-Christophe Bédard-Rubin, "L'émergence inattendue de la dualité institutionnelle à la Cour suprême du Canada depuis Pepin-Robarts" (2021) 29:2 Bulletin d'histoire politique 125–1 at 139. Examples include justices Rothstein and Major. See, for example, Christopher Bird, "Bilingualism Is Good, but It's Not Everything", *The Court.ca* (August 13, 2008), online: http://www.thecourt.ca/judicial-bilingualism-is-good-but-its-not-every

DOI: 10.4324/9781003279112-8

The justices' bijural legal training also contributes to the Court's distinctiveness.[8] In Quebec, private law is governed by the civilian tradition that can be traced back to France's *Napoleonic Code*, which is derived from Roman law.[9] In the other provinces, private law is governed by England's common law tradition, which is rooted in case law and precedential reasoning.[10] To be clear, Indigenous law applies to various legal areas that involve the rights and interests of Indigenous Peoples – a legal system that existed prior to Canada's colonization by France and England.[11] But the justices are not legally required to be tri-jural, let alone bijural.[12] Some justices are trained exclusively in the civil law tradition, others solely in common law, and some in both.[13] Until the recent nomination of Justice O'Bonsawin in 2022, none of the Court's justices were Indigenous.[14]

Canada's pluralistic legal landscape generates important implications.[15] The common law system governs public law disputes between the state and individuals in all provinces, such as in administrative law and in criminal law.[16] In contrast, the private law system is civilian in Quebec and tied to the common law in the other provinces.[17] Justices who lack legal training and knowledge in one type of legal system still resolve its disputes, interpret its laws, and draft decisions that shape its application. They do so even though some concepts that are fundamental in one legal system – such as consideration in common law contract law – do not exist in the other.[18]

---

thing/; Bédard-Rubin and Rubin, "The Elusive Quest for French on the Bench", *supra* note 2 at 260–261.

8 Rosemary Cairns Way, "Reforming Judicial Appointments: Change and Challenge" (2017) 68 UNBLJ 18 at 27.

9 John E.C. Brierley, "The Renewal of Quebec's Distinct Legal Culture: The New Civil Code of Quebec" (1992) 42:4 UTLJ 484 at 488–489.

10 Louis LeBel and Le Saunier, "L'interaction du droit civil et de la common law à la Cour suprême du Canada" (2006) 47:2 C de D 179 at 181.

11 Brian Thom, "Encountering Indigenous Law in Canada" in Foblets et al., eds, *The Oxford Handbook of Law and Anthropology* (Oxford: Oxford University Press, 2022) at 114–116.

12 See, for example, Matthew Shoemaker, "Bilinguisme et Bijuridisme à la Cour suprême du Canada" (2012) 35:2 Revue Parl Can 30 at 31.

13 Ibid. at 30–32; Adrian Popovici, "Le Rôle de la Cour suprême en droit civil" (2000) 34:3 RJT 607.

14 Nick Boisvert, "Michelle O'Bonsawin Becomes 1st Indigenous Person Nominated to Supreme Court of Canada" *CBC News* (August 19, 2022), online: https://www.cbc.ca/news/politics/michelle-obonsawin-scc-nomination-1.6556152.

15 Deborah Cao, *Translating Law* (Toronto: Multilingual Matters, 2007) at 66.

16 Marc Cuerrier, Sandra Hassan, and Marie-Claude Gaudreault, "Canadian Bijuralism and Harmonization of Federal Tax Legislation" (2003) 51:1 Can Tax J 133 at 136.

17 Ibid.

18 Cao, *Translating Law*, *supra* note 13 at 66.

Previously, scholars have conducted empirical studies that examine how legal pluralism and linguistic capacities shape adjudication on the Supreme Court of Canada. Some have explored how unilingualism affects panel composition and decision-making.[19] Others have shown how the Supreme Court cites Anglophone authors far more frequently than their Francophone counterparts.[20]

Using descriptive statistics, this chapter analyses the language of doctrinal sources – such as books, law review articles, and governmental reports – that the justices cite in private law decisions that originated in Quebec versus in other provinces. It focuses on Supreme Court of Canada decisions in the areas of tort law, contract law, and property law. This chapter's results show that the Court rarely cited French-language doctrinal sources in private law decisions that originated outside of Quebec, and rarely cited English-language doctrinal sources in cases that originated in Quebec. It demonstrates that cases that originated in Quebec tend to have the highest rate of bilingual doctrinal sources. These results also lay the groundwork for future empirical research that can explain why courts disproportionately cite English versus French doctrinal sources in certain cases.

5.2 Bilingualism and Private Law Pluralism

The nexus between bilingualism and bijuralism at the Supreme Court matters for various reasons. Begin with bilingualism. Francophones constitute a minority group within Canada.[21] According to 2022 statistics, English is the first language of roughly 75% of Canada's population, while French is the first language of approximately 22% of that population.[22] Only 18% of the country's population speak both official languages.[23]

Bilingualism requirements in courts – including at the Supreme Court of Canada – aims to fulfil various objectives.[24] First, bilingualism requirements aim to ensure equality of status for official language minorities and

---

19 See, for example, Bedard-Rubin and Tiago Rubin, "Assessing the Impact of Unilingualism", *supra* note 3.
20 Peter McCormick, "The Judges and the Journals: Citation of Periodical Literature by the Supreme Court of Canada, 1985–2004" (2004) 83:3 Can B Rev 633 at 653–655.
21 Statistics Canada, "While English and French Are Still the Main Languages Spoken in Canada, the Country's Linguistic Diversity Continues to Grow" (Ottawa: Statistics Canada, 2022) at 2. Available at: https://perma.cc/UFS4-RAZP.
22 Ibid.
23 Ibid.
24 For an overview of bilingualism's importance in adjudication, see: Bédard-Rubin and Rubin, "The Elusive Quest for French on the Bench", *supra* note 2 at 254–256.

support their development.[25] The Court has recognized that language plays a fundamental role "in human existence, development, and dignity", and "bridges the gap between isolation and the community".[26] Language rights, for their part, aim to protect and preserve official language minorities' language and culture.[27]

Second, bilingualism seeks to maximize mutual comprehension between the speaker (or writer) and their audience, which can promote fairness in legal disputes.[28] Language barriers characteristically undermine individuals' capacities to express themselves, understand others, and be understood by others. Typically, interpreters bridge this gap. Yet functional bilingualism can allow a reader or listener to understand linguistic nuances that can be lost through an interpreter's translation.[29] Simultaneous translations may also contain significant mistakes that alter the speaker's conveyed message and how the listener understands it.[30] Bilingualism increases one's ability to discern these nuances and understand others without the need for a medium.

Third, bilingualism can help ensure that legal decisions better incorporate official language minorities' perspectives. Unilingualism limits the pool of doctrinal resources from which judges draw.[31] Judges who do not understand French secondary sources are unlikely to read them, use their arguments, or cite them.[32] Nor can unilingual Anglophone judges under-

---

25 *R v Beaulac,* [1999] 1 SCR 768 at para. 20, citing: *Official Languages Act,* RSC 1985, c 31 (4th Supp), s 2.

26 Pierre Foucher, "Le juge et la gouvernance linguistique" in *La Gouvernance Linguistique: Le Canada en Perspective* (Ottawa: Les Presses de l'Université d'Ottawa, 2005) at 142. Citing: *Re Manitoba Language Rights,* [1985] 1 SCR 721 at 744; Leslie Green, "Are Language Rights Fundamental?" (1987) 25:4 Osgoode Hall LJ 639 at 651.

27 *R v Beaulac,* [1999] 1 SCR 768 at paras 25, 41.

28 Denise Réaume, "Official Language Rights: Intrinsic Value and the Protection of Difference" in Kymlicka and Norman, eds, *Citizenship in Diverse Societies* (Oxford: Oxford University Press, 2000) at 255 (providing an overview of natural rights-based conceptions of language rights).

29 Jayesh M. Rathod, "The Transformative Potential of Attorney Bilingualism" (2013) 46:3 U Mich JL Reform 863 at 879, 885. Although Rathod focuses on attorney bilingualism, similar arguments apply to the judiciary.

30 Sébastien Grammond and Mark Power, *Should Supreme Court Judges Be Required to Be Bilingual?* (Kingston: Institute of Intergovernmental Relations, 2011) at 4–5; Ralph Kaplan, "Breaking through the Language Barrier" (1954): 27:6 J Educational Sociol 278 at 279.

31 Grammond and Power, *Should Supreme Court Judges Be Required to Be Bilingual, supra* note 28 at 4-5, cited in: Bédard-Rubin and Rubin, "The Elusive Quest for French on the Bench", *supra* note 2 at 254–255, 261; Amanda Simard, "Understanding Both Official Languages at the Supreme Court of Canada" in Carstairs, ed., *Pages of Reflection: A Journal of Essays by Senate Pages,* Vol. 3 (Ottawa: 2020) at 25.

32 See, for example, Grammond and Power, *Should Supreme Court Judges Be Required to be Bilingual, supra* note 28 at 4–5.

stand French language case law or written arguments.[33] Unilingual judges
can thus overlook important doctrinal contributions that can improve the
quality of their judicial decisions, and ultimately, the law.[34]

Bijuralism exacerbates these problems. Supreme Court justices decide
disputes that involve a private law system in relation to which they lack
formal legal training and expertise.[35] As discussed above, certain basic
concepts exist in one legal system but not the other.[36] Furthermore, the
mode of reasoning and the hierarchy of sources differs between both legal
systems as well.[37] Statutory law is the primary source of law in a civil law
system, whereas case law fulfils that role in the common law.[38]

The overlap between unilingualism and unijuralism results in important asymmetries. Some scholars note that only Anglophone Supreme
Court of Canada justices have been unilingual, which disadvantages parties whose words cannot be directly understood.[39] Francophone scholars
experience a different form of hindrance: they are less likely to be cited
by the Court compared to their Anglophone counterparts (more on this
below).[40] The disparity may be particularly stark for scholars who write
in areas other than civil law. French-language treatises in areas of public
law – such as criminal law and procedure, constitutional law, or administrative law – are cited less frequently by courts outside of Quebec compared to English-language treatises.[41] These disparities may incentivize
Francophone authors to write in English to increase the likelihood that
they will be cited, which can further decrease French-language research
and scholarly publications.[42]

---

33 Michel Doucet, "Le bilinguisme : une exigence raisonnable et essentielle pour la nomina-
    tion des juges a la Cour suprême du Canada" (2017) 68 UNBLJ 30 at 31, citing: Gram-
    mond and Power, *Should Supreme Court Judges Be Required to be Bilingual*, *supra* note 28.
34 Grammond and Power, *Should Supreme Court Judges Be Required to Be Bilingual*, *supra*
    note 28 at 4–5.
35 Shoemaker, "Bilinguisme et Bijuridisme", *supra* note 10 at 32–33.
36 Cao, *Translating Law*, *supra* note 13 at 66.
37 Shoemaker, "Bilinguisme et Bijuridisme", *supra* note 11 at 32–33; Jean-Louis Baudouin,
    "*Quo* Vadis" (2005) 46:1-2 C de D 613 at 622–623.
38 LeBel and Le Saunier, "L'interaction du droit civil et de la common law", *supra* note 8 at 181.
39 Juan JiménezSalcedo, "Le débat autour du bilinguisme des juges à la Cour suprême du
    Canada : analyse de la doctrine et des débats parlementaires" (2020) 33 Int J Semiot Law
    325 at 333, footnote 25 in the text.
40 Grammond and Power, *Should Supreme Court Judges Be Required to Be Bilingual*, *supra*
    note 28 at 9.
41 Vaughan Black and Nicholas Richter, "Did She Mention My Name: Citation of Academic
    Authority by the Supreme Court of Canada, 1985–1990" (1993) 16:2 Dalhousie LJ 377
    at 394. Also cited in Grammond and Power, *supra* note 28.
42 See, for example, Pierre Frath, "L'enseignement et la recherche doivent continuer de se
    faire en français dans les universités francophones" (2011) 13 APLV langues modernes 1
    at 4–5.

However, a bilingualism or bijuralism requirement for Supreme Court of Canada justices could result in other consequences. Such a requirement could exclude a large portion of racialized or Indigenous Supreme Court of Canada nominees who are unilingual or unijural.[43] Thus, an increase in linguistic or jural diversity could decrease diversity and representation in other respects.

5.3 Existing Empirical Studies: SCC Bilingualism and Bijuralism

Scholars have conducted empirical studies that examine how legal training and language capabilities affect Supreme Court adjudication. In a series of articles, Jean-Christophe Bédard-Rubin and Tiago Rubin explored how unilingual justices impact case outcomes in various respects, such as panel composition, assertiveness, and deference.[44] Their dataset (which was compiled initially by Benjamin Alarie and Andrew Green) comprised Supreme Court of Canada decisions between 1985 and 2013 in one study,[45] and from 1969 to 2013 in another.[46] Note that Alarie and Green's dataset was larger and included decisions between 1954 and 2013.[47] Bédard-Rubin and Rubin's studies were limited to Supreme Court decisions that dealt with federal law, such as Aboriginal law, constitutional law, and criminal law.[48]

Their research demonstrated that the panel size for Quebec cases was smaller for all areas of law compared to the panel size of cases from other provinces, and that unilingual Anglophone justices were less likely to sit on Quebec cases compared to bilingual ones.[49] Their results further indicated that unilingual Anglophone justices are less likely to write a

---

43 Nasager, "The Supreme Court, Functional Bilingualism, and the Indigenous Candidate", *supra* note 4 at 799; Olivia Stefanovich, "Bilingualism Requirement for SCC Justices Creates 'Needless Barrier' for Indigenous Candidates, Critics Say" CBC News (March 31, 2021).

44 Bédard-Rubin and Tiago Rubin, "The Elusive Quest for French on the Bench", *supra* note 3 at 259–264; Bedard-Rubin and Tiago Rubin, "Assessing the Impact of Unilingualism", *supra* note 3 at 736–750.

45 Bédard-Rubin and Tiago Rubin, "The Elusive Quest for French on the Bench", *supra* note 2 at 257.

46 Bedard-Rubin and Tiago Rubin, "Assessing the Impact of Unilingualism", *supra* note 3 at 731.

47 Ibid.

48 Bédard-Rubin and Tiago Rubin, "The Elusive Quest for French on the Bench", *supra* note 2 at 256; Bedard-Rubin and Tiago Rubin, "Assessing the Impact of Unilingualism", *supra* note 3 at 736.

49 Bedard-Rubin and Tiago Rubin, "Assessing the Impact of Unilingualism", *supra* note 3 at 737, 739.

solo opinion in Quebec cases compared to cases from other provinces.[50] Bédard-Rubin and Rubin's research showed that bilingual justices were more likely to write an opinion in cases that came from Quebec compared to cases from other provinces.[51] Lastly, they demonstrated that the Court's level of bilingualism has increased since 1985 as more functionally bilingual justices have been appointed.[52]

Other scholars have examined how Supreme Court of Canada justices cite English versus French doctrinal sources. Vaughan Black and Nicholas Richter examined who the justices cited in their decisions issued between 1985 and 1990.[53] Black and Richter divided each decision into individual and co-authored judgments (meaning judicial opinions), so they could better identify which judges cited which doctrinal sources.[54] Their research indicated that the rate at which decisions cited doctrinal sources tripled between 1957 and the period between 1986 and 1990.[55] Furthermore, although civil law justices cited doctrinal sources less frequently than common law justices, civil law-related judgments had more citations than common law judgments.[56]

Peter McCormick conducted an empirical study that examined the most frequently cited authors and law review articles between 1985 and 2004.[57] The study demonstrated that the top ten most cited authors were exclusively Anglophone, and that the most cited law review articles were largely written in English.[58] Building on that research, Sébastien Grammond and Mark Power note that the justices cite Anglophone doctrine seven times more than Francophone doctrine.[59]

Another study by Peter McCormick and Tammy Praskach showed that between 1984 and 1993, Supreme Court of Canada justices from Quebec were roughly ten times more likely to cite to Quebec lower-court judicial decisions than justices from other provinces.[60] McCormick and Praskach attribute this disparity predominantly to the justices' language

---

50 Ibid. at 741–743.
51 Ibid. at 744–747.
52 Bédard-Rubin and Tiago Rubin, "The Elusive Quest for French on the Bench", *supra* note 2 at 261; Bédard-Rubin, "L'émergence inattendue", *supra* note 5 at 139.
53 Black and Richter, "Did She Mention My Name", *supra* note 39 at 378–379.
54 Ibid. at 378.
55 Ibid. at 383.
56 Ibid. at 387–388.
57 McCormick, "The Judges and the Journals", *supra* note 18 at 653–656.
58 Ibid.
59 Ibid.
60 Peter McCormick and Tammy Praskach, "Judicial Citation, the Supreme Court of Canada, and the Lower Courts: A Statistical Overview and the Influence of Manitoba" (1996) 24:2 Man LJ 335 at 353.

and experience rather than the applicable legal system.[61] Notably, they suggest that the imbalance does not stem from the civil law itself since so few Supreme Court of Canada appeals involve Quebec private law.[62]

5.4 Methodology and Dataset

This chapter examines new research questions regarding the doctrinal sources that Supreme Court of Canada justices cite in private law decisions. Using quantitative techniques, it explores the extent to which the justices cite French, English, and bilingual doctrinal sources in decisions that originated in Quebec versus in other provinces.

This chapter employed the following three-step methodology to gather descriptive statistics. In the first step, research assistants manually compiled a dataset of all Supreme Court of Canada decisions between 2000 and 2020 related to three areas of private law: contract, tort, and property law. To do so, they accessed the Supreme Court of Canada's decisions via its online database, which provides a chronological list of each decision that the court issued in a particular year.[63] The research assistants manually analysed the official keywords and summaries of the Court's decisions to determine whether they involved the areas of contract, tort, or property law. The decisions that fell within these areas of private law were inserted into an Excel spreadsheet as part of the dataset. The dataset also included each decision's province of origin. The co-author, Skolnik, then manually reviewed the summary of the decisions provided by the research assistants to ensure that they were sufficiently connected to the areas of contract, tort, or property law. Decisions with a sufficiently strong connection to these areas of private law were included in the dataset.

In the second step of the methodology, a research assistant entered the doctrinal sources mentioned in each of these decisions into the Excel spreadsheet, and classified these doctrinal sources into English, French, and bilingual categories. The doctrinal sources that the Court cites are listed under the heading "authors cited" of each decision. Doctrinal sources include, for example, secondary sources such as books, law review articles, governmental reports, and legal dictionaries. For each decision, the research assistant also indicated the percentage of English, French, and bilingual doctrinal sources cited in each decision given the total number of doctrinal sources that the Court cited within it. The research

---

61 Ibid. at 354.
62 Ibid.
63 See: Supreme Court of Canada, "Supreme Court Judgments". Available online at: https://decisions.scc-csc.ca/scc-csc/scc-csc/en/nav_date.do.

assistant classified the language of doctrinal sources in the following way. Notably, they examined the official English and French version of each decision to cross-reference how the Court cited the language of each doctrinal source. Unilingual sources maintained the same document name in both English and French versions of the Supreme Court decisions. In contrast, the document name varied for bilingual sources in the English and French versions of the same decision. Using this method, the research assistant identified the language of each doctrinal source.

In the third step, a research assistant coded the province of origin (Quebec versus the rest of Canada) and the language of each doctrinal source (English, French, or bilingual) for each decision within the dataset. This data was also entered in the Excel spreadsheet. The data was coded to produce charts that illustrate the extent to which justices cite English, French, or bilingual doctrinal sources in cases that originated in Quebec versus in the rest of Canada.

This dataset ultimately comprised 100 Supreme Court of Canada decisions issued between 2000 and 2020. Within that dataset, 73 of the Court's decisions included citations to five or more doctrinal sources. For analyses that examined the ratio of French-language to English-language citations within individual decisions, only decisions with five or more distinct citations were used.

This chapter's methodology has certain limitations. First, the initial manual screening of decisions may have overlooked relevant cases that should have been included in the dataset. Second, the methodology's initial step was not a purely objective process. The research assistants and co-authors exercised judgment regarding which decisions they included within the dataset. This judgment was necessary because the relationship between a decision and these three areas of private law varied in intensity. The co-authors decided that the strength of the connection between the decision and contract, tort, or property law determined whether the decision was included within the dataset. Decisions with stronger connections to these areas of law – meaning the decision's principal legal issues related to contract, tort, or property law – were incorporated into the dataset. In contrast, decisions with weaker or more tenuous connections to these areas of law were excluded from it. Admittedly, other scholars may have interpreted the strength of the connection between the decision and private law differently. For this reason, they may have included different decisions within the dataset, or excluded different decisions from it. Third, this chapter's dataset did not include certain areas of private law – such as labour law or family law – that may have produced different results.

5.5 Results and Discussion

The descriptive statistics gathered through this project deepen our understanding of Supreme Court decision-making in several respects. To begin with, these results provide new insight into the language of doctrinal sources that the justices cite in private law decisions that originated in Quebec versus in other provinces. This project produced the following findings.

This chapter's first finding is that in private law decisions that involve five or more citations to doctrinal sources, the justices rarely cite French-language doctrinal sources when the decision originated outside of Quebec, especially when compared with the frequency with which English-language doctrinal sources are cited in cases that originated in Quebec. Of the 73 decisions with five or more citations to doctrinal sources, 35 originated in Quebec, while the remaining 38 originated in the rest of Canada. Among the 38 decisions that originated outside of Quebec, only four of these decisions – or roughly 11% of the 38 decisions originating outside of Quebec – cited to at least one French-language doctrinal source. In contrast, among the 35 decisions that originated in Quebec, 26 of these decisions – or 74% of the 35 decisions that originated in Quebec – cited to at least one English-language doctrinal source.

Figure 5.1 illustrates this first finding. Each bar in the chart represents a single decision. The colour composition of each bar represents the portion of that decision's citations that are from English-language, French-language, or bilingual sources (black, dark grey, and light grey, respectively). A white gap has been added to the chart to better distinguish the province of origin for each decision; decisions that originated in Quebec are to the right of the gap, while decisions that originated in the rest of Canada are to the left of the gap.

Figure 5.2 shows the occurrence of French-language and English-language citations in each private law decision with five or more doctrinal sources, which are represented in terms of raw numbers rather than ratios. Decisions that originated in Quebec are highlighted in grey, whereas decisions that originated in other provinces are highlighted in white. English-language doctrinal citations are represented by a black bar and French-language doctrinal citations are represented by a grey bar.

Like Figure 5.1, Figure 5.2 demonstrates how private law decisions that originated in Quebec are much more likely to cite English-language doctrinal sources compared to how frequently decisions that originated in the rest of Canada cite to French-language doctrinal sources. Decisions that originated in Quebec that cite to English-language sources are represented by black bars in the grey background area. In contrast, decisions that originated outside of Quebec that cite to French-language doctrinal sources are represented by grey bars in the white background

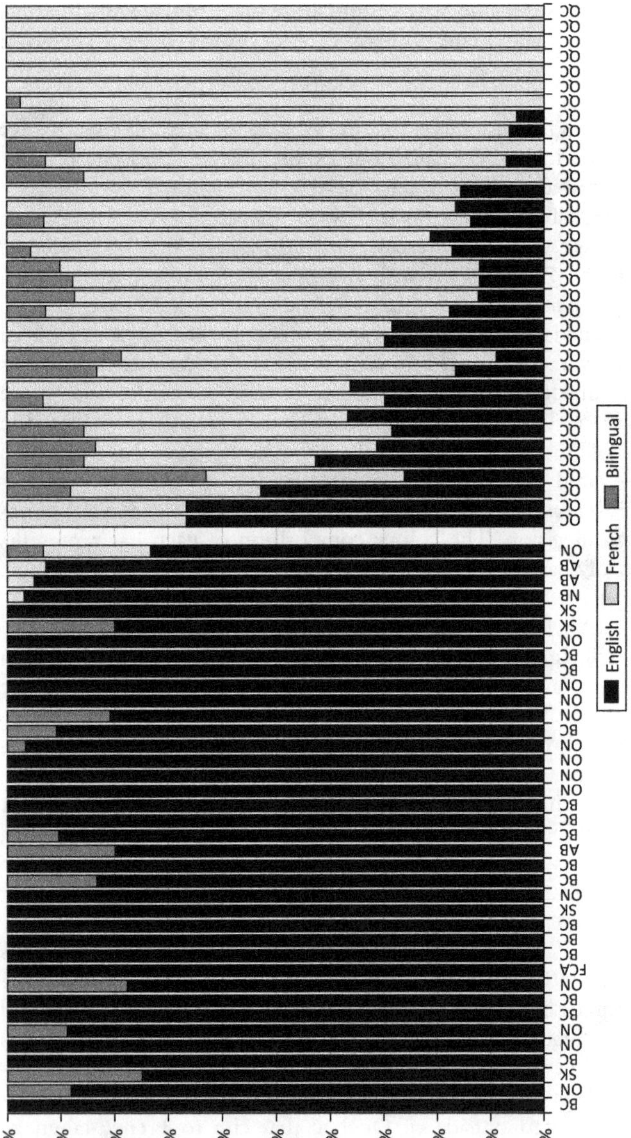

Figure 5.1 French-Language citations as a % of all citations

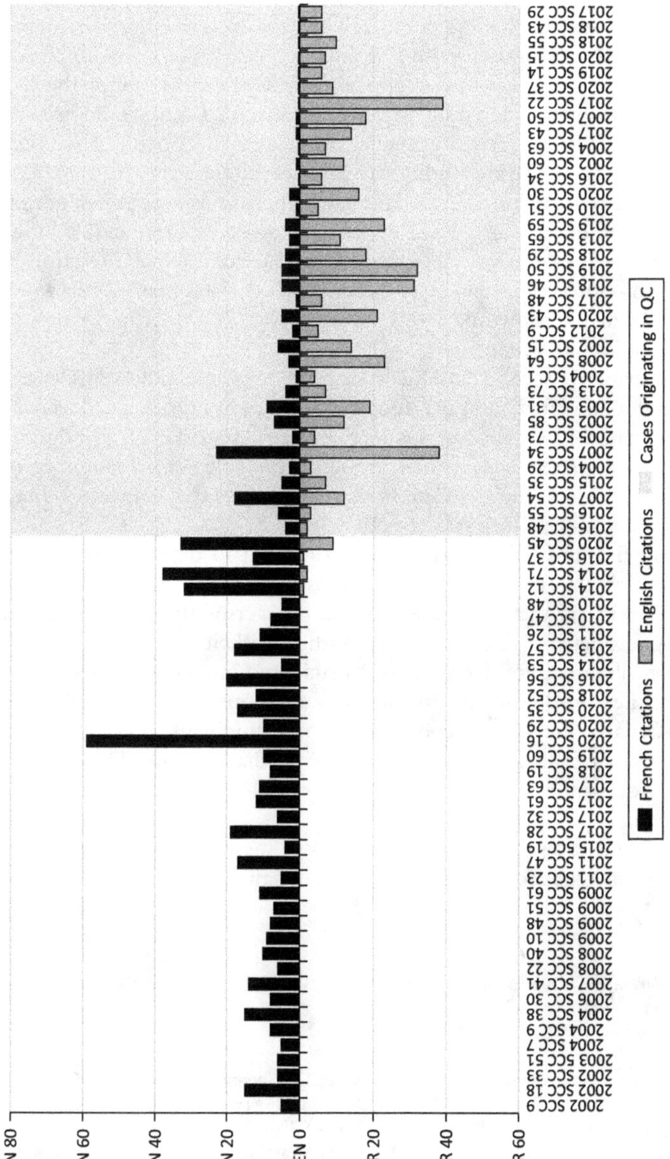

Figure 5.2 Number of English vs. French citations

area. Moreover, Figure 5.2 shows the low absolute numbers of citations involved. Only two decisions have ten or more citations to both English- and French-language sources; both originated in Quebec.[64]

Figure 5.1 and Figure 5.2 show that the justices do occasionally cite French-language sources in certain private law decisions that originated outside of Quebec and that involve five or more citations to doctrinal sources. *Callow v. Zollinger*, on appeal from Ontario, is one of the few notable non-Quebec decisions that *do* cite French-language doctrine.[65] Similarly, *Bhasin v. Hrynew*, which originated in Alberta, also cites French-language doctrine, though to a lesser extent than *Callow*.[66] But the Court's reliance on French-language doctrine is somewhat unsurprising in these decisions. Notably, the decisions incorporated a long-standing civil law concept – the duty to exercise contractual discretion in good faith – into common law contract law.[67] For this reason, it is to be expected that judges would cite Quebec private law doctrine, much of which is written in French.

This chapter's second finding is that the Supreme Court of Canada more frequently cites bilingual doctrinal sources in private law decisions that originated in Quebec versus in the rest of Canada. This finding is particularly interesting given that French is the sole official language of Quebec.[68] Beyond Quebec, Ontario is the province that is most likely to cite bilingual sources (see Figure 5.1).

Figure 5.3 and 5.4 analysed data from all 100 decisions that form this chapter's dataset. Figure 5.3 demonstrates how Supreme Court of Canada decisions that originated in Quebec versus the rest of Canada (RoC) cite doctrinal sources that are either in their non-dominant language or bilingual. For decisions that originated in Quebec, English was coded as the non-dominant language. For decisions that originated in the rest of Canada, French was coded as the non-dominant language. While the right side of the table represents decisions that originated in Quebec, the left side of the table represents decisions that originated in the rest of Canada.

Figure 5.3 shows that more than 65% of the dataset's decisions that originated in Quebec cited to an English-language doctrinal source. By

64 *Dell Computer Corp. v Union des consommateurs,* 2007 SCC 34; *Bruker v Marcovitz,* 2007 SCC 54.

65 *C.M. Callow Inc. v Zollinger,* 2020 SCC 45.

66 *Bhasin v Hrynew,* 2014 SCC 71.

67 Krish Maharaj, "*Callow* in More Ways than One: The Supreme Court Causes More Confusion in Contract" (2021) 53:1 Ottawa L Rev 53 at 85; Terry Skolnik, "Precedent, Principles, and Presumptions" (2021) 54 UBC L Rev 935 at 947.

68 *Charter of the French Language,* CQLR c C-11, preamble; *An Act respecting French, the official and common language of Québec,* SQ 2022, c 14.

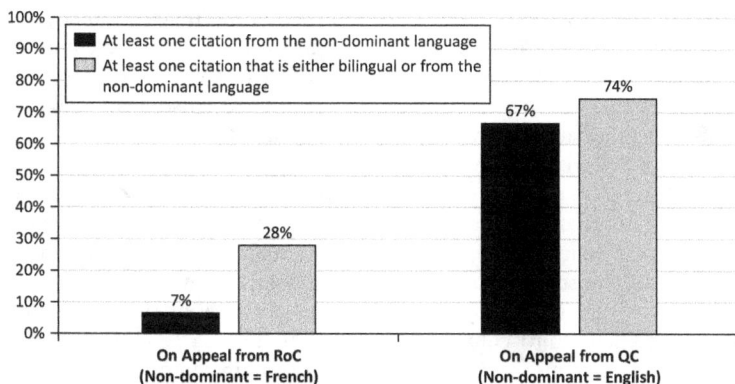

Figure 5.3 Citations form the non-dominant language

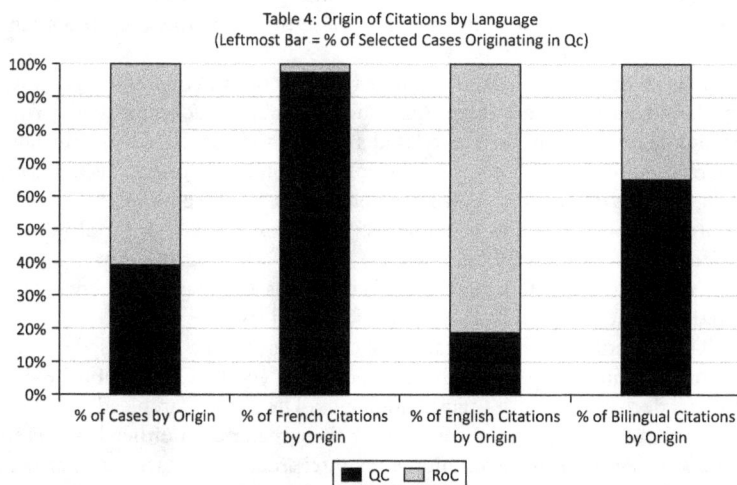

Figure 5.4 Origin of citations by language

comparison, less than 7% of the dataset's decisions that originated in the rest of Canada cited to a French-language doctrinal source. When bilingual sources are added, the gap is less significant but remains stark: 74% of decisions that originated in Quebec cited to an English or bilingual source, while decisions that originated in the rest of Canada cited to French or bilingual sources only 28% of the time.

Figure 5.4 demonstrates the extent to which the province of origin is correlated with the language of citation: English, French, or bilingual. Citations from decisions that originated in Quebec are represented by a black bar, while citations from decisions that originated in the rest of Canada are represented by a grey bar. This table illustrates that decisions that originated in Quebec disproportionately cite French-language sources and bilingual sources.

In Figure 5.4, the leftmost column represents the portion of decisions in our dataset that originated in Quebec versus the rest of Canada, which establishes a benchmark against which the other three columns can be compared. The second column shows that more than 97% of citations to French-language doctrinal sources occur in decisions that originated in Quebec. The third column shows that citations to English-language sources are much more common in cases that originated outside Quebec, though almost 20% of citations to English-language sources are found in decisions that originated in Quebec. Lastly, the fourth column shows that citations to bilingual sources are more common in cases that originated in Quebec. Notably, 65% of citations to bilingual sources are in Quebec-origin decisions, despite the fact that these decisions make up less than 40% of the dataset.

This chapter's two salient findings raise important concerns regarding the language of private law scholarship. Notably, academics who write French-language scholarship related to common law-based private law are rarely cited in such cases.[69] These Francophone scholars' insights, in turn, are not incorporated into the common law's development through Supreme Court of Canada decisions.[70] The reverse is true for English-language Quebec private law scholars. Notably, their scholarship may not be cited in Supreme Court of Canada decisions and may not be incorporated into the Court's development of the civil law.

These findings are especially important given the Court's demonstrated commitment to bilingualism. For instance, the Court publishes its judicial decisions in both official languages. The parties can plead in either official language, and they can submit their material in either language, too. Translators provide simultaneous interpretation services so that the public can understand Supreme Court of Canada hearings. However, the Court's decisions tend to cite doctrinal sources in only one official language – English or French – depending on whether the case originated in Quebec versus in the rest of Canada.

---

69 Grammond and Power, *Should Supreme Court Judges Be Required to Be Bilingual, supra* note 28 at 4–5.

70 Ibid.

This project's research findings reinforce the need to promote bilingualism through the language of doctrinal sources that the justices cite in decisions that originated outside of Quebec. Justice system actors could help mitigate these problems in different ways. For instance, legal organizations could create a website or online database that would provide a list of French-language doctrinal sources related to common law private law. In the knowledge that Francophone and bilingual sources are generally overlooked in cases that originated outside of Quebec, the justices could aim to incorporate a greater number of these sources into their decisions. Francophone legal organizations, for their part, could intervene at higher rates in private law decisions that originated outside of Quebec – and include French-language doctrine within their *facta* – in light of the risk that the justices will not cite French-language doctrinal sources in their decision.

5.6 Conclusion

This chapter employed descriptive statistics to explore an important aspect of the Supreme Court of Canada's adjudication in private law decisions: the language of doctrinal sources that the justices cite. This research produced the following two important findings. First, in private law decisions that involve five or more citations, the Court rarely cites French-language doctrine in cases that originated outside of Quebec, especially when compared to the frequency with which the Court cites English-language doctrine in cases that originated in Quebec. Second, in contrast to private law decisions that originated in the rest of Canada, private law decisions that originated in Quebec disproportionately cite bilingual sources and sources in the province's non-dominant language: English.

This project's research findings also lay the groundwork for future research. Notably, quantitative techniques can help identify trends related to how the justices cite certain doctrinal sources. For instance, subsequent projects can evaluate whether the justices are increasingly – or decreasingly – citing to French and bilingual sources, including in decisions that originated in Quebec versus the rest of Canada. Moreover, future numerical analyses can provide additional insight into which justices cite English, French, or bilingual doctrinal sources.

Furthermore, this chapter's findings do not explain why the Court disproportionately cites French-language doctrine in cases that originated in Quebec, and English-language doctrine in cases that originated in other provinces – a research question that merits further scrutiny. For instance, do these disparities simply reflect that there are more available English-language common law doctrinal sources than French ones, and more French-language civil law doctrinal sources than English ones? Do the parties' and intervenors' *facta* primarily cite doctrinal sources in one of the official languages despite the availability of other doctrinal sources in the other official language? Or does the Court prefer to cite doctrinal sources in one official language even when presented with doctrinal sources in the other official language? Future statistical analysis may provide important answers to these questions.

Part 3
Changing Judicial Practice

6 The Supreme Court of Canada Leave Project

A Dataset and Machine Learning Model for Predicting Leave Application Outcomes

Paul-Erik Veel and Katie Glowach

6.1 Introduction

While much of this book is focused on appeals heard by the Supreme Court of Canada (SCC), most cases never get to the Supreme Court. The primary barrier is the leave application process. For the majority of cases, the Court must grant leave (permission) for cases to be heard, and the likelihood of getting leave in any case is low. In a typical year, the Supreme Court refuses to grant leave in 90% or more of cases in which it is sought.

In this chapter, we introduce Lenczner Slaght's Supreme Court of Canada Leave Project.[1] This project consists of a database that contains dozens of datapoints pertaining to every single leave application decided by the Supreme Court of Canada from January 1, 2018, onward. This dataset allows us to glean a variety of insights into the operation of the Supreme Court as an institution. We have also used this dataset to build a machine learning model – in essence, an algorithm that learns based on known training data, which is in turn used to make predictions regarding new data – to predict the likelihood of cases getting leave to the Supreme Court of Canada. While this type of tool is not commonly used in legal practice at present, which makes benchmarking performance difficult, this model has significant predictive utility and compares favourably to some commonly used screening tools in other practical domains such as medicine.

---

1 A more fulsome description of the project and other associated content can be found at https://litigate.com/data-driven-decisions.

DOI: 10.4324/9781003279112-10

6.2 An Overview of Seeking Leave to Supreme Court of Canada

In broad terms, the Supreme Court of Canada has jurisdiction over three kinds of cases: 1) federal references that go directly to the Supreme Court[2] (advisory opinions issued by the Supreme Court in response to particular questions posed by the federal government); 2) appeals in which there is an appeal "as of right" to the Supreme Court of Canada,[3] in which case a litigant can automatically bring an appeal to the Supreme Court, and 3) appeals in which the Supreme Court has granted leave to appeal.[4]

Cases to which the Court has granted leave are a particularly important subset of the Court's work, for several reasons. First, quantitatively, most cases heard by the Supreme Court of Canada are cases in which the Court has granted leave to appeal. Each year between 2012 and 2019, between 65% and 84% of the Supreme Court's docket consisted of cases in which the Court granted leave to appeal. The number of by leave cases heard by the Court dropped significantly in 2020 and 2021, likely as a consequence of the COVID-19 pandemic. But even in those years, by leave cases still represented over half the Supreme Court's docket.[5]

Second, cases in which the Supreme Court grants leave tend to be more jurisprudentially significant than cases that reach the Court as of right. For cases heard by leave, the Supreme Court has affirmatively decided, pursuant to the requirements of the *Supreme Court Act*, that the case raises sufficiently significant issues that it warrants being heard. By contrast, appeals by right lack any screening mechanism that would ensure that they raise jurisprudentially significant issues. Consistent with this, a recent study by one of the co-authors of this chapter found that most decisions from the bench – that is, decisions rendered without substantial reasons on the same day the appeal was heard – have been issued in decisions in which the Court heard the case as of right.[6] Consequently, the likelihood of the Court rendering full reasons that will ultimately

---

2 *Supreme Court Act*, RSC 1985, c S-26, s 53.

3 These include provincial references determined by provincial Courts of Appeal, as well as various criminal appeals. See *Supreme Court Act*, RSC 1985, c S-26, s 36; *Criminal Code*, RSC 1985, c C-46, ss 691–693.

4 *Supreme Court Act*, RSC 1985, c S-26, s 40. There are also provisions by which the provincial courts and the Federal Court of Appeal can grant leave for a case to be heard by the Supreme Court of Canada: *Supreme Court Act*, RSC 1985, c S-26, ss 37–37.1. However, this power is rarely invoked.

5 Supreme Court of Canada 2021 Year in Review, available at: https://www.scc-csc.ca/review-revue/2021/index-eng.html.

6 Alex Bogach, Jeremy Opolsky, and Paul-Erik Veel, "The Supreme Court of Canada's From-the-Bench Decisions", (2022) 106 SCLR (2d) 251–287.

make a case jurisprudentially significant is much higher for cases in which the Court has granted leave.

Finally, in most subject matters, effectively all the Court's jurisprudence consists of cases in which the Court has granted leave. For several decades, the Court's as of right jurisdiction has been limited to certain classes of criminal cases – those in which there is a dissent at the intermediate appellate court on a question of law, or those in which the intermediate appellate court has overturned an acquittal and substituted a conviction – as well as appeals of provincial references. Consequently, essentially every civil decision rendered by the Court over the last several decades occurred because the Supreme Court first granted leave.

The *Supreme Court Act* sets out the test for leave in s 40(1).[7] This provision contains two requirements for the Supreme Court to exercise its by leave jurisdiction. First, the decision below must be a decision of the "Federal Court of Appeal or of the highest court of final resort in a province". In most cases, this means either a provincial appellate court or the Federal Court of Appeal. However, in some cases in which there is no right of appeal to a provincial appellate court – for example, with respect to publication bans in criminal cases – leave may be sought from the decision of a provincial Superior Court.[8]

Second, the decision must be "by reason of its public importance or the importance of any issue of law or any issue of mixed law and fact involved in that question, one that ought to be decided by the Supreme Court or is, for any other reason, of such a nature or significance as to warrant decision by it". This is typically referred to as the "public importance" requirement. This requirement is the primary gatekeeper in most cases in which leave to appeal is sought to the Supreme Court of Canada. In practice, the "public importance" requirement means that the Court decides which cases it thinks are significant enough to warrant being heard. The Supreme Court does not typically issue reasons explaining why it did or did not grant leave to appeal.

Importantly, the Court grants leave in only a small minority of cases in which leave is sought. According to the Supreme Court's Year in Review 2021, in 2020 the Court granted 34 leave applications (approximately 8% of those filed) and dismissed 383 (approximately 92% of those filed). While the precise percentage varies from year to year, over the last five years the Supreme Court has consistently granted leave in less than 10%

---

7 *Supreme Court Act*, RSC 1985, c S-26, s 40(1).
8 *Dagenais v Canadian Broadcasting Corp.*, [1994] 3 SCR 835 at 858–862.

of cases in which leave has been sought.[9] Over the last ten years, the high-water mark for leave being granted was just under 13% in 2012.[10]

6.3 The Value of Quantitative Analysis of SCC Leave Applications

Supreme Court of Canada leave applications decisions are different from the appeal and reference decisions that form the subject of other chapters of this text, primarily because there are almost never reasons issued in leave applications. Consequently, the methods described in other chapters of this book, such as natural language processing tools or citation analysis, are not applicable to analysing Supreme Court of Canada leave application decisions. Instead, as described below, an analysis of Supreme Court leave applications must proceed on the basis of labelled leave application data.

Yet these same reasons also make a quantitative analysis of the Supreme Court's leave application process valuable. In appeals in which reasons are rendered, the possibilities of natural language processing and citation analysis compete with the conventional legal approach of closely reading a case. Such conventional reasoning will generally yield significant insights. Where a Court renders reasons for its decision, it provides a set of general principles that can be applied to future cases. Careful analysis through the conventional tools of legal reasoning can provide strong indications of how courts will rule in a range of future cases. While there will always be "hard" cases that may not be determined solely by reference to past decisions or other legal authorities, the existence of reasons will at the very least narrow the set of such "hard" cases.

By contrast, in leave applications, none of these methods work, because of the absence of reasons. Perhaps as a consequence, the leave process, and leave decisions have historically been understudied by the legal academy. A search of typical legal sources yields only a handful of academic articles pertaining to the leave process or outcomes.[11] Perhaps for similar

9 Supreme Court of Canada 2021 Year in Review, available at: https://www.scc-csc.ca/review-revue/2021/index-eng.html.

10 Supreme Court of Canada 2021 Year in Review, available at: https://www.scc-csc.ca/review-revue/2021/index-eng.html.

11 See, for example, Bertha Wilson, "Leave to Appeal to the Supreme Court of Canada" (1983) 4:1 Advoc Q 1; Geoff R. Hall, "Applications for Leave to Appeal: The Paramount Importance of Public Importance" (1999) 22:1 Advoc Q 87; Bruce Ryder and Taufiq Hashmani, "Managing Charter Equality Rights: The Supreme Court of Canada's Disposition of Leave to Appeal Applications in Section 15 Cases, 1989–2010" (2010) 51 SCLR (2d); Denise Cooney, "An Absence of Reason: Why the Supreme Court of Canada Should Justify Dismissing Applications for Leave to Appeal" (2012) 70:1 UT Fac L Rev

reasons, when legal practitioners have tried to predict whether cases will get leave, their predictions have been limited to vague and imprecise heuristics, such as the observation that cases that raise constitutional issues are relatively more likely to get leave.

As such, our collective knowledge regarding the leave process is limited. For example, Netolitzky has done valuable work exploring the difficulties that self-represented litigants face in getting leave to the Supreme Court.[12] Ryder and Hashmani found that, from the late 1990s onward, the rate of successful leave applications in cases raising equality rights under s 15 of the Charter had dropped, and governments generally had better prospects of obtaining leave than parties seeking to advance equality rights.[13] This prior work provides valuable insights into leave applications in very particular contexts, but it does not provide general insights into leave applications as a whole.

There is significant value in better understanding the leave application process and outcomes. As described above, the leave process is the gatekeeper for most of the Court's jurisprudence, and the vast majority of its jurisprudentially significant decisions. Understanding how and why cases come to be at the Supreme Court of Canada has implications for the evolution of that Court's jurisprudence. For practitioners, the stakes are also significant. Various factors may motivate clients to seek leave, such as an attempt to preserve their liberty, child protection or custody issues, or significant financial considerations. Yet the costs of seeking leave can be significant. While we are not aware of any study quantifying the costs of leave applications, they range from thousands to tens of thousands of dollars, depending on the particular practice area and lawyers' rates. However, the likelihood of success on a leave application is low, on average. Improving our understanding of what factors drive leave decisions could lead to better screening by lawyers in relation to whether it is worth seeking leave in a particular case. Screening out even a modest percentage of leave applications on the basis that they have no reasonable prospect of

---

41; Donald J. Netolitzky, "The Walking Wounded: Failure of Self-Represented Litigants in 2017 Supreme Court of Canada Leave to Appeal Applications" (2021) 58:4 Alta L Rev. 837; "Justice Suzanne Côté's Reputation as a Dissenter on the Supreme Court of Canada" SCLR: Osgoode's Annual Constitutional Cases Conference 88. (2018) (suggesting that the leave process may have changed as a result of Justice Côté).

12 Donald J. Netolitzky, "The Walking Wounded: Failure of Self-Represented Litigants in 2017 Supreme Court of Canada Leave to Appeal Applications" (2021) 58:4 Alta L Rev 837.

13 Bruce Ryder and Taufiq Hashmani, "Managing Charter Equality Rights: The Supreme Court of Canada's Disposition of Leave to Appeal Applications in Section 15 Cases, 1989–2010" (2010) 51 SCLR (2d).

success could save millions of dollars annually in expenses to litigants, let alone the effort and expense saved by the Court as an institution.

6.4 The Supreme Court of Canada Leave Project

We at Lenczner Slaght have sought to fill this gap in knowledge of leave applications with our Supreme Court of Canada Leave Project. The project consists of a hand-coded dataset of information pertaining to every leave application decided by the Supreme Court of Canada from January 1, 2018, onward.[14] Our database is updated with new cases as they are released each week.

In our database, we collect four categories of information about every leave application:[15]

1. Information about the parties – For example, the names of the parties, the number of applicants and respondents, information about what type of player each party is (e.g. individual, corporation, government, etc.), each party's role in the litigation (e.g. plaintiff vs defendant), and whether they were represented by counsel in their Supreme Court leave application.
2. Information about the case – For example, the general area of law into which the case falls, whether it is a class action, and whether the case is also proceeding as of right.[16]
3. Information about the lower court decision – For example, which Court decided the decision below, whether there was a dissent or concurrence at the court below, whether the intermediate appellate court overturned another lower court decision, whether there were

---

14 There is no particular significance to starting the dataset as of January 1, 2018. Our goal was that, before the project was first put to use in early 2021, we wanted to have at least 1,500 leave decisions in our dataset, including at least 100 cases in which leave was granted. We felt that this would provide a large enough set. We determined that we could meet those criteria by including all cases from January 1, 2018, onward. While, in general, more data is better, it is highly labour-intensive to build such a database manually, so we limited how far back we went.

15 All of the data in our database is obtained by a human review of publicly available sources. The sources consulted are: 1) the Supreme Court of Canada's news releases, published on https://scc-csc.lexum.com/; 2) case information from the Supreme Court of Canada's website at https://www.scc-csc.ca/; and 3) decisions of lower courts.

16 In the majority of appeals as of right, the Supreme Court's jurisdiction arises from the fact that the case is a criminal law matter where there was a dissenting judge at the Court of Appeal. However, in those cases, the Supreme Court will only hear an appeal as of right on the particular issue(s) on which a judge dissented at the Court of Appeal. Consequently, if an appellant who has an appeal as of right wishes to raise issues other than the issues on which a judge dissented, they must seek leave to appeal in respect of those issues.

interveners, how many judges decided the decision below, the length of the decision, the number of citations to other legal sources in the decisions, the number of days of argument, and the length of time it took to decide the case.

4. Information about the leave process pertaining to that case – For example, the date of the decision below, the date that leave was applied for, and the date the leave application was decided. These data points allow us to explore seasonality effects (e.g. whether the Court is more likely to grant leave in particular months) as well as autocorrelation effects (e.g. whether there is some temporal relationship between successful leave applications). These data points also allow us to generate other variables, such as the number of leave applications decided on any particular day.

As of September 1, 2022, our dataset contained information about dozens of different variables for 2,234 leave decisions.

6.5 Insights from the Data

We put that dataset to two broad uses. The first involved extracting general insights about the leave process and outcomes at the Supreme Court of Canada. As a simple example, we use this data to understand how long it takes for leave applications to be decided at the Supreme Court of Canada. Our data shows that in 2021, the median time from application to decision was 136 days (approximately four and a half months). This is one metric that can be helpful in evaluating the Court's performance over time and advising clients.

While just knowing a median is helpful, knowing the full distribution of timelines to decision is usually more helpful. Figure 6.1 depicts a histogram of the time from Supreme Court leave application to decision in 2021. The bin widths are 30 days: that is, each bar represents the number of cases decided within increasing 30-day periods from the date the leave application was filed. This shows that the distribution is wide. Figure 6.1

This data shows that it is not unusual for cases to be decided more quickly or more slowly. Indeed, 22% of leave applications decided in 2021 took more than six months to be decided, and 5% of leave applications took more than ten months to be decided. This data can be relevant to parties considering whether to pursue a leave application.

Going a step further, we also use our dataset to relate facts about the leave process to leave outcomes. For example, some Supreme Court watchers have commented on social media in relation to a phenomenon

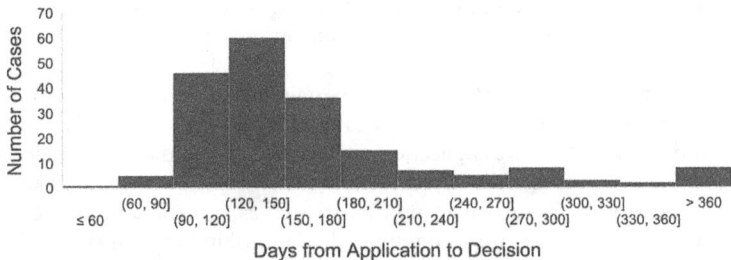

Figure 6.1 SCC leave applications - days from application to decision

at the Supreme Court that they have labelled "clearing the decks":[17] in essence, the Court has a tendency to decide, from time to time, a disproportionately large number of leave applications on a single day and to dismiss most or all of them. Our dataset allows us to empirically investigate whether this phenomenon does exist. Interestingly, it does: the likelihood of a randomly selected case being granted leave depends on the number of other leave applications being decided on the same day. To put it in concrete terms, over our entire dataset (up to September 1, 2022), leave applications decided on days on which ten or fewer cases were being decided had a 10.6% chance of being granted leave, while leave applications decided on days on which 20 or more cases were being decided had just a 4.7% chance of being granted leave.[18] Notably, this "clearing the decks" effect persists even after we control for other variables that impact the likelihood of leave being granted.

Finally, our dataset allows us to test whether certain factors impact the likelihood of cases getting leave to the Supreme Court of Canada. We had hypothesized that a variety of factors might be associated with a higher likelihood of getting leave and, indeed, we found that a number of strong associations were in line with our hypotheses. Without describing all of our findings in detail – which would be beyond the scope of this chapter – below are some of the main conclusions we reached.

First, we found that indicators of disagreements at the courts below were associated with an increased likelihood of leave being granted. Thus, the Court of Appeal allowing the appeal from the lower court's

17 See, for example, @jopolsky, February 24, 2022, "Big week with 14 leave applications. Another instance of clearing the decks?"; @jopolsky, March 17, 2022, "As predicted. 15 up. 15 down. Clearing the decks indeed".

18 Using a difference in proportion test, the difference between two is statistically significantly greater than 0 at the p<0.001 level.

decision, as well as the presence of dissents and concurrences at the Court of Appeal, were each associated with a higher probability of the Supreme Court granting leave. This is not surprising: a case in which different judges disagreed on the outcome is more likely to be associated with an underlying legal issue of public importance.

Second, indicators that the Court of Appeal perceived a case as having increased importance or complexity were also associated with an increased likelihood of the Supreme Court granting leave. For example, we found that, all else being equal, longer reasons, more citations to other sources, and a longer period of time under reserve at the Court of Appeal were each associated with an increased likelihood of the Supreme Court granting leave.

Third, we had speculated that in criminal cases, the Supreme Court was more likely to grant leave in cases in which the Crown seeks leave, rather than in cases in which the accused seeks leave.[19] This hypothesis turned out to be well founded: Crown applications for leave were more likely to be granted than applications by criminal defendants, and this effect persisted and remained significant even after controlling for other variables.

Finally, and unsurprisingly, the self-representation of an applicant in a leave application was strongly associated with leave not being granted. Indeed, in our entire dataset between January 1, 2018, and September 1, 2022, the Supreme Court did not grant leave in a single case in which the applicant was self-represented on the leave application.

Yet not all of our hypotheses turned out to be well founded. First, many Supreme Court watchers would likely predict that it is easier to get leave in cases that raise certain types of legal issues (for example, constitutional law cases). We have found little evidence that area of law by itself, after controlling for other factors, has a substantial impact on the likelihood of getting leave.[20]

19 There are several different reasons why this might be true. It may be that the Supreme Court of Canada more seriously entertains requests from the Crown to hear cases than it does from criminal defendants. It may be that the Crown is more selective in seeking leave – that is, it tends to seek leave relatively more often in those cases that are likely to get leave. Or it may be that cases in which the Crown seeks leave somehow otherwise implicate the public interest to a greater extent on average than do cases in which defendants seek leave.

20 There may be more complex relationships between the nature of the legal issues at play in the case and the likelihood of getting leave. Indeed, our current black-box machine learning model for predicting the likelihood of leave applications being granted, described below, does include some features relating to the legal issue at play in a case. This suggests that area of law does factor into the likelihood of a case getting leave, but not in a simple way.

Second, we had hypothesized that class action cases were more likely to get leave. Class actions tend to be large cases – both in terms of the quantums at stake and the number of persons affected. Moreover, they often raise complex procedural and substantive issues. Consequently, it seemed reasonable that they would be relatively more likely to get leave to appeal. However, we found no evidence that class actions were statistically significantly more likely to get leave to the Supreme Court of Canada than other types of cases, after controlling for other factors.

Finally, we had conjectured that it might be easier to obtain leave to appeal from decisions of some provincial courts of appeal than others. For example, there are three judges from Ontario and three from Quebec on the Supreme Court of Canada, and we might have therefore expected that they would form a critical mass of judges who would have a greater interest in cases originating in those provinces. However, we have found no evidence to date of any difference in the likelihood of leaving being granted based on the province of origin of a case.

6.6 Our Supreme Court of Canada Leave Prediction Model

While these insights help us understand the Supreme Court institutionally, the second use to which we put our dataset is more practical: predicting the likelihood that particular cases will get leave to the Supreme Court of Canada. A well-performing model for predicting the likelihood that particular cases will get leave has significant potential utility in practice. Such a model could be used as a first pass screening mechanism: that is, it could identify a subset of cases with a sufficiently low chance of getting leave that no further analysis would be warranted. Such a model could also provide a second opinion function. If a lawyer judges that a case has a high likelihood of being granted leave, but the model predicts a low probability, that may lead one to investigate further to decide whether a leave application is worth it. By contrast, if the predictive model is aligned with the lawyer's opinion, that is a datapoint that supports the reasonableness of the lawyer's opinion. Finally, a model can provide a quantitative prediction. While some clients may want a probability estimate of their chances of getting leave, lawyers may have difficulty formulating their advice in probabilistic terms. A predictive model could help ameliorate that situation.

With those goals in mind, we built a machine learning model that learns from the existing data in the dataset to predict the probabilities of new cases getting leave. A machine learning model is, at its most general, any algorithm that builds a model by learning on the basis of pre-existing training data, which is then used to make predictions regarding other test data.

Machine learning models can take various forms. Relatively simple statistical models, such as ordinary least squares regression (for continuous data) and logistic regression models (for binary outcomes), can be considered machine learning models when built on the basis of a set of training data and then applied to test data. Such models are simple and easily interpretable, because there is some form of linear relationship between the input variables and the output. Readers will have no doubt seen the simplest form of linear regression, which is simply a straight line drawn through a cloud of data points in a way that best approximates a relationship between two variables. On the other end of the spectrum are blackbox models. These are machine learning models that may make more accurate predictions, but at the expense of interpretability; the complex relationships of the variables and how they relate to each other are determined by an algorithm and cannot be understood by humans, even those who design the models.[21]

The outcomes of leave applications are a binary variable: a party either gets leave, or it does not. Machine learning models that predict what category a particular case will fall into are called classification models. However, in our model, we do not predict the binary outcome of whether or not a case will get leave. Rather, the output of our model is the *probability* that a particular case will get leave. We believe probability predictions are more useful than a simple yes/no prediction, as probabilities can be more easily combined with lawyers' judgments to render an overall assessment of the likelihood that a case will get leave.

When we present such data publicly, we often group cases into four categories:

1. Cases to Watch – These are cases in which our model predicts a greater than 25% chance that leave will be granted. The chance that these cases will be granted leave is much better than average. While cases included in this category will not all get leave, they are worth watching as strong candidates.
2. Possible Contenders – These are cases in which our model predicts between a 5% and 25% chance that leave will be granted. These cases have an average to somewhat above-average chance of getting leave.

---

21 Full details of such black-box models are beyond the scope of this chapter, but examples include Random Forest models (which attempt to aggregate the results of hundreds or thousands of randomly constructed decision trees on subsets of the training data) and neural network models (which are inspired by the information-processing approach used by neurons in the human brain). For a fulsome discussion of various machine learning algorithms, see Max Kuhn and Kjell Johnson, *Applied Predictive Modeling* (New York: Spring Science+Business Media, 2013).

While most cases in this category will not get leave, we expect to see a healthy minority of cases in this category being granted leave.

3. Unlikely Contenders – These are cases in which our model predicts between a 1% and 5% chance that the case will get leave. The safe bet is against leave being granted in these cases, but we do expect to see leave being granted from time to time.

4. Long-Shots – These are cases in which our model predicts a less than 1% chance that the case will get leave. Although it will happen from time to time, it would be a significant outlier for our model for these cases to be granted leave.

While the particular probabilities that form the boundaries of these categories are arbitrary, such categories can be helpful in guiding lawyers' reasoning. For example, it would not be unreasonable for a lawyer to apply a heuristic that they presumptively recommend seeking leave to appeal in any Cases to Watch, while presumptively recommending against seeking leave to appeal in any Long-Shots. Cases falling into the intermediate categories may be worth further consideration, taking into account the lawyer's own judgment of the likelihood of success as well as the stakes of the case.

We have applied different machine learning models to our leave application data at different times. For example, the primary model we used for predictions between October 2021 and March 2022 was a logistic regression model with 11 independent variables. This model performed reasonably well in making predictions. Moreover, because of the ease of conventional statistical analysis with a logistic regression model, we were able to gain insights into the factors that impact the likelihood of leave being granted, including what factors are statistically significant and what the effect size is. That model helped us identify several factors that were statistically significantly associated with getting leave to the Supreme Court, many of which are described above.

However, as of April 2022, we began to use a gradient-boosting model for our predictions, as implemented in the R package *xgboost*. *Xgboost* is a commonly used open-source machine learning package whose powerful performance in a variety of contexts has been recognized.[22] Our current model (as of September 1, 2022) is trained on 16 variables in the dataset. Based just on those 16 variables, our model performs strongly.

The "performance" of machine learning models can be difficult to assess in an intuitive manner. This is particularly true when the variable of

---

22 In brief, *xgboost* is an ensemble learning method that uses an iterative series of decision trees in a way that can take a set of individually weak variables and combine them into a strong model overall.

interest is a binary variable that is very unbalanced (that is, one outcome occurs substantially more often than the other). In such cases, of which Supreme Court of Canada leave decisions are an example, accuracy (or how often a prediction is correct) can be an unhelpful measure. For example, if only 8% of cases get leave, a model that predicts that no case will ever get leave is accurate 92% of the time. While that sounds like a very accurate model, that metric is essentially useless in practice.

A better way of thinking about model performance in those circumstances is to consider the trade-off in a model between sensitivity and specificity. Sensitivity refers to the true positive rate: how often the model correctly identifies a case as likely to get leave, when it actually does get leave. Specificity refers to the true negative rate: how often the model correctly identifies a case as not likely to get leave, when it in fact does not get leave. There is invariably a trade-off between sensitivity and specificity in any given model: the more true positives the model correctly predicts, the more false positives it will likely predict as well.

One measure of the performance of a machine learning model in classification problems that combines both of these measures is known as the area under the curve (AUC). As the name suggests, the AUC measures the area under a particular curve, the Receiver Operator Characteristic (ROC) curve. The ROC curve provides a plot of a model's sensitivity vs 1 minus sensitivity at every threshold value. The AUC of a model ranges between 0.5 and 1, with values closer to 1 indicating a better model. An AUC of 0.5 indicates that the model has no predictive power; put simply, it is no better at predicting than flipping a weighted coin. By contrast, an AUC of 1.0 indicates a perfect model with both 100% sensitivity and 100% specificity.[23] An AUC of 1.0 is impossible in any real-world context. However, the classical description holds that an AUC between 0.7 and 0.8 is acceptable, an AUC between 0.8 and 0.9 is excellent, and an AUC above 0.9 is outstanding.[24] By way of comparison, the Framingham risk score, a tool used in medicine for predicting the likelihood of certain cardiovascular events, has been reported to have a real-world AUC of between 0.62 and 0.78.[25]

As of September 2022, our predictive model, built using *xgboost*, when trained on 70% of the data (randomly selected) and then used to predict the remaining 30%, has an AUC in the range of 0.85. This shows that our

---

23 In contrast to a naïve measure like accuracy, ROC curves and AUC curves are insensitive to disparities in the proportions of the different classes: Max Kuhn and Kjell Johnson, *Applied Predictive Modeling* (New York: Spring Science+Business Media, 2013) at 264.

24 D.W. Hosmer and S. Lemeshow, Chapter 5, *Applied Logistic Regression*, 2nd ed. (New York: John Wiley and Sons, 2000), pp 160–164.

25 See, for example, Asaf Bitton and Thomas Gaziano, "The Framingham Heart Study's Impact on Global Risk Assessment" Prog Cardiovasc Dis. 2010; 53(1): 68–78.

machine learning classification model has significant utility in predicting the outcomes of leave applications. The strong performance of our model is not based on being able to directly measure whether a case raises issues of public importance. Rather, our model works because we have successfully identified a range of factors that correlate, to various degrees, with cases that the Supreme Court considers to be of public importance.

Our model is not, and never will be, perfect in predicting outcomes, for several reasons. First, our model does not incorporate all the data that is important in determining the outcome of leave applications. For example, our model does not presently incorporate any information about the quality of the leave application; assuming that the quality of lawyering matters even slightly to the likelihood of leave being granted, our model does not take this into account. We hope to be able to expand our dataset in the future to include such information. Second, even with access to every conceivable piece of information, our model would still almost certainly not be perfect, because it is modelling the behaviour of a small number of human beings. While the social sciences have shown us that human behaviour demonstrates regular patterns that can be modelled, such models will never be perfect. The fact that a model is not perfect does not mean it is not useful. In this case, there is good evidence that our model performs well enough to be a useful complement to lawyers' predictions.

6.7 Conclusion

The standard for being granted leave to appeal to the Supreme Court of Canada is the nebulous "public importance" standard. As a discretionary standard applied by a Court that does not provide any reasons for its decision, the leave application decision process is opaque. Yet that does not mean that leave application decision-making is devoid of patterns or completely unpredictable. On the contrary, our dataset has allowed us to identify several factors that are statistically correlated with getting leave to the Supreme Court. Our machine learning model, using just 16 variables, provides sufficient predictive insights to be useful as either a screening tool or a second opinion. We hope to improve the model's performance in the future through the collection of additional data.

7 The Supreme Court of Canada and Mainstreamed Judicial Analytics

Jena McGill and Amy Salyzyn[1]

7.1 Introduction

The Canadian legal community faces important questions about how to respond to the fast-growing field of judicial analytics. Although analysing judicial decision-making is not new, existing judicial analytics tools allow for faster and more powerful analyses of large amounts of information. In the short to medium term, these tools will likely improve in terms of technological capacity, quality of outputs, and accessibility.

In a previous work, we traced how the advent of "mainstreamed judicial analytics" could result in "a world where technology allows us to instantaneously draw up a detailed profile of a judge's past behaviour with a click of a smartphone button", resulting in unprecedented public insight into judges and the work of judging.[2] We considered the potential impacts of this development on the public's knowledge of the judiciary, the work of lawyers and how judges perceive and perform their work.[3]

In this chapter, we build on that prior work to address a narrower question: how might mainstreamed judicial analytics impact the Supreme Court of Canada? Specifically, we consider how analytics could influence: (1) the appointment process for Supreme Court judges; (2) the adjudication of cases at the Supreme Court; and (3) the ability of the public – and the Court itself – to appraise trends and tendencies in judicial decision-making at the Supreme Court.

We conclude that, given the public interest in the Supreme Court of Canada, mainstreamed judicial analytics tools will likely be used to

---

1 Jena McGill and Amy Salyzyn are professors at the Faculty of Law, University of Ottawa. For helpful feedback, the authors are grateful to Jacquelyn Burkell, Jon Khan, and colleagues at the Legal Data Science and the Supreme Court of Canada Workshop held at the University of Ottawa on September 30, 2022. University of Ottawa law student Ka Chi Wong provided helpful research assistance through the Centre for Law and Technology's 2022 Technoship Program.
2 Jena McGill and Amy Salyzyn, "Judging by the Numbers: Judicial Analytics, the Justice System and Its Stakeholders" (2021) 44(1) Dal L J 249 at 252.
3 Ibid. at 263–277.

DOI: 10.4324/9781003279112-11

scrutinize the Court and its judges. However, certain institutional features unique to the Court, including the fact that the Court sits in a panel and operates as an apex court (and therefore often engages in novel legal analyses), will limit, or render impossible, certain uses of judicial analytics. For example, it would be challenging to predict the substantive outcome of any individual case by drawing on patterns from the Court's previous decisions or from patterns in lower court decisions.

However, judicial analytics tools can be used for analyses that do not involve predicting case outcomes. For example, descriptive analysis of certain Court-level trends is possible. Patterns relating to leave applications, voting alignments, treatment of doctrine, and sources cited could all be examined by analytics tools. Profiles of Supreme Court justices could be used in recusal motions or, even earlier, at the appointments stage. Oral hearings could be mined for patterns, and written reasons could be examined for readability.

These possible uses of analytics hold promise in terms of their potential to increase the transparency and accountability of the Supreme Court's work. They also prompt important foundational questions about the Court and the work of judging. What makes a "good" Supreme Court judge? What kinds of observed patterns in Court practices should lead to reforms and why? What are the limits of the empirical study of patterns in the Court's work? What are the costs of shifting towards greater reliance on analytics data in the Supreme Court context?

Throughout the analysis that follows, we underscore the importance of "good" data. Judicial analytics tools that are poorly designed or supplied with incomplete or poor-quality inputs risk producing results that mislead users. As judicial analytics tools become cheaper to create and deliver, these sorts of quality-control issues will become increasingly important. Additionally, judicial analytics outputs must be properly contextualized and interpreted in order to be meaningfully understood. Accurate outputs are not, in themselves, sufficient. Data and statistical literacy are also necessary to ensure that judicial analytics technologies are responsibly deployed.

7.2 Towards Mainstreamed Judicial Analytics

Before turning to the Supreme Court context, this part provides a brief outline of judicial analytics.

The term "judicial analytics" refers to tools that use advanced technological techniques, such as machine learning, network analysis, and natural language processing, to analyse patterns in court data in order to gain insights into individual judges or courts. Currently, judicial analytics tools are primarily used by two groups: academics and litigators. Academic deployments often involve tools that are tailor-made for specific research projects focusing on a narrow question or set of questions.[4] Commercial tools designed for litigators are marketed as helping lawyers:

- "Find and use the precise case law language your judge relies on to craft arguments that will ring true to your judge."[5]
- "Get a sense of how long it will take to resolve [your] type of case in front of your judge."[6]
- "Take a deep dive into your judge's ruling tendencies on specific motions."[7]
- Understand "the personal factors that play a role in how [your judge] decides cases", including your judge's "net worth, education, work experience, political affiliation".[8]
- Monitor "outcome analysis by gender and race".[9]

Commercial analytics tools generally offer a comparative function, allowing an individual judge's decisions or behaviour to be compared to other judges or a court average.

To date, judicial analytics tools have been relatively difficult and expensive to create. Much court data is not digitized and, even where it is, it is not easy for machines to automatically analyse it. Judicial data is notoriously "unstructured": "a reported legal decision does not neatly organize relevant information into pre-set fields, unlike, for example, a well-designed electronic medical record".[10] This means that building judicial analytics tools has required significant manual work by humans,

---

4 Examples of such projects can be found in other chapters of this book. See, also, for example, Sean Rehaag, "Judicial Review of Refugee Determinations (II): Revisiting the Luck of the Draw" (2019) 45 Queen's LJ 1; and Sean Rehaag, "Luck of the Draw III: Using AI to Examine Decision-Making in Federal Court Stays of Removal", Refugee Law Lab Working Paper (January 11, 2023), ssrn: https://papers.ssrn.com/sol3/papers.cfm?abstract_id=4322881.

5 "Context", online: https://www.lexisnexis.ca/en-ca/products/context.page.

6 Ibid.

7 "Trellis", online: https://trellis.law/judge-analytics.

8 Robert Ambrogi, "New Judicial Analytics Product Predicts Motion Outcomes with Claimed 86.7% Accuracy" *LawSites*, online: https://www.lawnext.com/2022/07/new-judicial-analytics-product-predicts-motion-outcomes-with-claimed-86-7-accuracy.html.

9 See, for example, "Premonition Judicial Dashboard", online (pdf): *Premonition*, https://premonition.ai/wp-content/plugins/wonderplugin-pdf-embed/pdfjs/web/viewer.html?disabledownload=1&file=https%3A%2F%2Fpremonition.ai%2Fwp-content%2Fuploads%2F2018%2F01%2FPA036-Judicial-Dashboard-Sales-Sheet3.pdf/.

10 McGill and Salyzyn, *supra* note 1 at 260, drawing on a comparison made in Jon Khan, "The Life of a Reserve: How Might We Improve the Structure, Content, Accessibility, Length & Timeliness of Judicial Decisions?" (Master of Laws (LL.M) thesis, University of Toronto, Faculty of Law, 2019) [unpublished]), available online: https://tspace.library.utoronto. ca/bitstream/1807/98120/1/Khan_Jon_%20_201911_LLM_thesis.pdf.

including reading judicial decisions and inputting various data points. For example, *Lex Machina*, one of the earliest commercial legal analytics tools, required approximately 100,000 hours of human labour to "manually sort through, categorize, and correct the data" in order to develop its statistical database.[11] Another challenge is that court data is not automatically available in a useable form for this sort of analysis: getting "bulk access" to court data is key, but, traditionally, bulk access has been closely guarded by courts and only made available to select entities and researchers.[12]

However, three trends suggest that existing limitations are likely to ease in the near future. First, court data is increasingly digitized.[13] Second, there is a growing willingness by courts to make court-related data more accessible, including by providing bulk access.[14] Third, the technology used by analytics tools to read legal texts continues to improve.[15] Indeed, due to recent technological improvements, those with limited coding skills can analyse large quantities of legal texts with previously unknown ease and efficiency.[16] In view of these trends, we anticipate that judicial analytics will become mainstreamed in the short to medium term.[17] "Mainstreamed judicial analytics" refers to a world in which the general public has easy and inexpensive access to powerful judicial analytics tools. We imagine a reality in which detailed statistics about judges are available almost instantaneously to anyone, anywhere.

---

11 Tam Harbert, "The Law Machine", IEEE Spectrum 50:11 (2013) 31 at 34.

12 See, Sarah Sutherland, *Legal Data and Information in Practice: How Data and the Law Interact* (New York: Routledge, 2022) at 13 and Julie Sobowale, "The Right to Access Court Data", *CBA The National* (August 15, 2022), online: https://www.nationalmagazine.ca/en-ca/articles/legal-market/legal-tech/2022/the-right-to-access-court-data. See, also, Sean Rehaag, "Luck of the Draw III" *supra* note 3 at 28 (discussing the lack of bulk access to stay of removal decisions in the refugee context as a barrier to bringing computational methods to bear in this area).

13 See, for example, Jacquelyn Burkell and Jane Bailey, "Revisiting the Open Court Principle in an Era of Online Publication: Questioning Presumptive Public Access to Parties' and Witnesses' Personal Information" (2017) 48:1 Ottawa L Rev 147.

14 See, for example, Sobowale, *supra* note 11. For recent initiatives in relation to granting bulk access, see, for example, CanLII, "Call for Participants" (July 8, 2022), online: https://blog.canlii.org/2022/07/08/call-for-participants/.

15 See, for example, Sutherland, *supra* note 11 at 100 and Kevin Ashley, *Artificial Intelligence and Legal Analytics* (Cambridge: Cambridge University Press, 2017) at 4–5.

16 Sean Rehaag, "Luck of the Draw III" *supra* note 3.

17 McGill and Salyzyn, *supra* note 1 at 263.

7.3 Analytics at the Supreme Court of Canada

How might a world characterized by mainstreamed judicial analytics impact the Supreme Court of Canada? Below, we explore the potential influence of judicial analytics in three areas: the appointments process, the work of adjudicating cases, and the assessment of the Court's work.

7.3.1 Analytics and the Appointment Process

One possible output of mainstreamed judicial analytics tools is easily accessible, detailed statistical summaries of the judicial careers of applicants, or rumoured applicants, to the Supreme Court of Canada. Such summaries of judge-applicants could be used (1) by the media to report on applicants and/or (2) more formally, as part of the application and selection process for Supreme Court judges.

7.3.1.1 Applicant Data

The availability of statistical information on applicants will depend, of course, on the specifics of an applicant's career to date. Some applicants may not have any prior judicial experience. For those that do, however, we can imagine a world in which analytics tools offer detailed summaries of the past judicial decision-making patterns of many applicants to the Court.

Such summaries might include information about how appellate courts have treated the applicant's decisions or track favourable citations of an applicant's past cases.[18] Trends related to certain types of litigants could be identified, such as, for example, how often the judge ruled in favour of the Crown in criminal cases. More pointedly, analytics reports suggesting preference or bias in relation to litigants belonging to certain demographics or communities could be produced. A judge's workload, the amount of time they take to decide cases, or an evaluation of their writing could also be detailed.[19] All these statistics could be presented in a comparative format vis-à-vis other potential applicants or even current Court members.

---

18 For discussion of subsequent judicial citations, see, Stephen Choi and G. Mitu Gulati, "Choosing the Next Supreme Court Justice: An Empirical Ranking of Judge Performance" (2018) 78 S Cal L Rev 23.

19 With respect to evaluating judicial writing, see, for example, this LinkedIn post which reports on an analysis of the contents of Justice O'Bonsawin's prior judicial decisions: https://www.linkedin.com/posts/jurisage_filac-classification-of-obonsawin-judgments -activity-6966414340023320577-hbu8/?utm_source=share&utm_medium=member _ios.

7.3.1.2 Possible Uses of Analytics Data on Supreme Court Applicants

Media coverage of Supreme Court appointments generally relies on impressionistic and/or anecdotal accounts of the judicial records and tendencies of applicants.[20] Judicial profiles prepared using analytics tools could add statistical evidence to speculation about how an applicant might behave if appointed to the Court. Media coverage could highlight certain statistics or provide links to more robust statistical dashboards, similar to those tracking trades in professional sports. Indeed, these kinds of statistical reports are part of media coverage in other jurisdictions, including, for example, during the recent appointment of Justice Ketanji Brown Jackson to the United States Supreme Court.[21]

Judicial profiles generated by analytics tools might also come to play a role in the application and selection process for Supreme Court judges. Currently, applicants complete a 20-page questionnaire with information about their judicial, legal, educational, and personal backgrounds, as well as their perspectives on "the role of the judiciary in Canada's legal system".[22] Applicants are not required to provide quantitative information about their past judicial records (if applicable). Given the presumptive relevance of an applicant's past judicial work to their suitability for the Supreme Court, a future questionnaire could require applicants to include a statistical profile of any existing judicial decisions they have written.

---

20 See, for example, Kate Allen, "Michael Moldaver's Climb to Top Court Had Blue-Collar Beginnings", online: https://www.thestar.com/news/canada/2011/11/14/michael _moldavers_climb_to_top_court_had_bluecollar_beginnings.html (stating, in respect of former Justice Moldaver, that "[s]ome court watchers say he is particularly tough on defence lawyers"), and Tamsin McMahon, "Karakatsanis: Supreme Court's New Trend-Bucking Wild Card", online: https://nationalpost.com/posted-toronto/karakatsanis -supreme-courts-new-trend-bucking-wild-card (quoting Philip Slayton, in respect of Justice Karakatsanis: "[w]e are all creatures of our experience and our background and if you have been a government bureaucrat for a long time you tend to think like a government bureaucrat and you tend to favour the government bureaucracy ... It's just human nature").

21 See, for example, Adam Feldman, "Just the Stats: Ketanji Brown Jackson as a District Court Judge" (March 18, 2022), online: https://abovethelaw.com/2022/03/just-the -stats-ketanji-brown-jackson-as-a-district-court-judge/. For a Canadian example of a judicial dashboard, see Deliberate Legal Design, "Canadian Judges Database", online: https://www.deliberatelegaldesign.com/courts-judges-of-canada.

22 Office of the Commissioner for Federal Judicial Affairs, *Questionnaire for the Supreme Court of Canada Judicial Appointment Process 2022*, online: https://www.fja-cmf.gc.ca/ scc-csc/2022/pdf/Questionnaire-SCC-Judicial-Appointment-Process.pdf.

7.3.1.3 *Benefits and Risks*

Insights gleaned from analytics could increase transparency and provide more information for making and evaluating Supreme Court appointments. Supplementing impressionistic media accounts and self-reported applicant information with data-based evidence about judicial performance could contribute to a more complete picture of how an applicant behaves as a judge.

Of course, there are also risks to using analytics data in the appointments process. An analytics tool could generate "bad" information that is presented to the public and/or those involved in the appointment process. This could happen if a tool used an incomplete or erroneous dataset (the "garbage in, garbage out" problem) or generated statistics based on bad coding (that is, used the wrong math).[23] Moreover, even "correct" outputs can be misleading if their statistical salience is not properly explained[24] or if the reader does not have sufficient background knowledge about the justice system or the work of judging to appreciate the output in context. For example, a report detailing how often a judge has been appealed must be situated within a broader appreciation of the appeals process, including the reality that some appeals are by right and that being appealed is not necessarily evidence of "bad judging", even when an appeal is successful.[25]

The increased scrutiny of judges made possible by judicial analytics tools risks being used in a disproportionately negative or punitive way against applicants from equity-seeking groups. A parallel can be drawn with the differential media coverage of women and racialized candidates seeking public office in Canada. Research has indicated that this coverage, often disproportionately negative, not only diminishes the electoral prospects of these candidates but also serves to discourage members of these communities from seeking public office in the first place.[26] In the judicial appointments context, recent research reveals that women and racialized nominees to the Supreme Court of the United States are, during confirmation hearings, "pressed more heavily on their judicial philosophy, which is often a coded way of questioning their competence to serve on

---

23 McGill and Salyzyn, *supra* note 1 at 269.
24 For an example, see McGill and Salyzyn, *supra* note 1 at 269–270.
25 See, for example, *Phillips v Naamani*, [1998] QJ No. 2504 at para. 72 (observing, "[t]he fact that judges may be found to have erred in law and are reversed is certainly not indicative of negligence").
26 See, for example, Erin Tolley, "Racial Mediation in the Coverage of Candidates' Political Viability: A Comparison of Approaches" (2015) 41 J of Ethnic & Migration Studies 963 and Elizabeth Goodyear-Grant, *Gendered News: Media Coverage and Electoral Politics in Canada* (UBC Press, 2013).

the court".[27] Given the heightened scrutiny already faced by certain judicial applicants, new and more detailed information from judicial analytics tools could fuel additional attacks. The risk of judicial analytics outputs being "weaponized" against certain groups is worthy of sustained attention given Canada's pursuit of judicial diversity and the importance of treating all applicants fairly.[28]

To the extent that the appointment of Supreme Court of Canada justices ultimately rests in the political sphere,[29] one might also worry about analytics data being used in "policy litmus tests" for applicants. Such tests are a noticeable phenomenon in the United States, where parties and presidents make "promise[s] to appoint justices who will decide cases on a given policy in the direction favored by the party".[30] For example, several Republican party platforms include promises to appoint "law and order" judges.[31] It is possible that political actors could use judicial analytics tools to help them advance or choose applicants that seem to align with their policy preferences.

These benefits and risks suggest additional, more fundamental, questions about the appointments process. What makes a good Supreme Court judge? What makes for a good individual appointment given the other eight judges on the Court? Are a judge's past decisions necessarily indicative of how they will behave as a Supreme Court justice? What is the correct role, if any, for politics in the appointment process? These questions belie easy answers but are worthy of rich and serious discussion.[32]

---

27 Amelia Thomson-DeVeaux, "How Racism and Sexism Could Define Ketanji Brown Jackson's Confirmation Hearings" *FiveThirtyEight.com* (March 2, 2022), online: https://fivethirtyeight.com/features/how-racism-and-sexism-could-define-ketanji-brown-jacksons-confirmation-hearings/; see also Christina L. Boyd, Paul M. Collins Jr, and Lori A. Ringhand, "The Role of Nominee Gender and Race at U.S. Supreme Court Confirmation Hearings" (2018) 52:4 Law & Soc Rev 871.

28 Diversity is an express consideration in the Supreme Court appointment process. See, for example, the *Terms of Reference guiding the Independent Advisory Board for Supreme Court of Canada Judicial Appointments* at s.8(f), online: https://www.fja-cmf.gc.ca/scc-csc/2022/mandate-mandat-eng.html.

29 We note that the current process involves the Prime Minister making the final decision following consultation with various stakeholders (including politicians) on a shortlist of candidates that is submitted by an independent advisory committee (Office of the Commissioner for Federal Judicial Affairs Canada, "Supreme Court of Canada Appointment Process – 2022: Frequently Asked Questions", online: https://www.fja-cmf.gc.ca/scc-csc/2022/questions-eng.html).

30 Charles Cameron and Jonathan Kastellec, "The Litmus Test for a Supreme Court Nominee" Vox.com (July 5, 2018), online: https://www.vox.com/mischiefs-of-faction/2018/7/5/17532488/litmus-test-supreme-court-nominee.

31 Ibid.

32 To be sure, there is a long history of conversations about what makes a good judge and a strong Supreme Court. For a recent example, see David Butt, "To Build a Strong Supreme Court, We Must Look at the Big Picture" *The Globe and Mail* (August 26, 2022), online:

Although judicial analytics tools can reveal patterns in an applicant's prior judicial decision-making, they cannot indicate which patterns are relevant and why. Simply dumping data into the applications process would be unproductive and could undermine public confidence in the Court.

7.3.2 Analytics and Adjudication at the Supreme Court

Mainstreamed judicial analytics may also come to influence the adjudication of cases before the Supreme Court as litigators use analytics to gain strategic advantages.

7.3.2.1 Data about How a Judge Decides

Generally speaking, commercially available judicial analytics tools aim to provide information about a single judge's tendencies. A challenge in using analytics to profile an individual Supreme Court judge is that, unlike trial judges, Supreme Court judges always sit in a panel and their most prominent outputs – reasons for judgment – often reflect "group work".[33] Supreme Court reasons can be unanimous, or the judges may be divided in any number of ways between majority, concurring, and dissenting reasons. Additionally, reasons are circulated for feedback and may be the product of negotiations and compromises between justices.[34] Although a justice may be formally listed as *the* author of a decision, the work product is not theirs alone. Indeed, some judgments are even formally co-authored. Also, judicial law clerks or court lawyers may contribute to the language or content of reasons, depending on the judge.[35]

7.3.2.2 Using Analytics Data in Adjudicating Cases at the Supreme Court

This "group work" dynamic is incompatible with the use of judicial analytics tools to profile individual Supreme Court judges with a view to helping one's case by tailoring *facta* or other court materials. Even if

---

https://www.theglobeandmail.com/opinion/article-to-build-a-strong-supreme-court-we-must-look-at-the-big-picture/. Our suggestion is simply that these conversations need to be linked to uses and potential misuses of data in the appointment process.

33 Emmett Macfarlane, *Governing from the Bench* (Vancouver: UBC Press, 2013) at 101 (observing, "the Supreme Court of Canada is a highly collaborative institution, and a true understanding of the development of its decisions requires an account of group interaction").

34 Ibid.

35 Ibid. at 106–108. See, also, Lorne Sossin, "The Sounds of Silence: Law Clerks, Policy Making and the Supreme Court of Canada", (1996) 30 UBC L Rev 279.

one could filter out a single justice's preferences within this collaborative context, the utility of such information would be limited, at best. Any profiled justice would be joined by several (usually eight) others in hearing and deciding a case, all or any of whom could have preferences that compete with or contradict those of a profiled justice.

One might imagine a judicial analytics tool tailored to the Supreme Court context that aims to "profile the bench" as a whole in order to predict the outcomes of individual cases. However, gathering a reliable set of data upon which to base Court-level predictions presents significant challenges. The Supreme Court decides a limited number of cases, across a huge breadth of subject areas. Further, the Court's status as an apex court creates a barrier to predictive uses. The Court is empowered to, and often does, establish new legal ground in its decisions, muting the value of past patterns in predicting future outcomes. The decision-making dynamic at the Court is very different to the trial level, where a judge's work must be connected to prior legal precedents.

That said, narrower use cases for judicial analytics in the Supreme Court context may exist. For example, it is possible to obtain general information about what sorts of judicial authorities or secondary sources the Court tends to rely on.[36] A lawyer could use this data to make more informed decisions about what to cite in their factum. Likewise, a litigant who knows about trends in the Court's decisions on leave to appeal applications could make an evidence-based choice about whether to seek leave in their case.[37]

Data from oral hearings could also yield insights for litigators. For example, in the United States, studies show that the party that is asked the most questions in a Supreme Court hearing is more likely to lose the case.[38] This type of analysis is now easier to do thanks to AI-empowered automatic transcription tools.[39] More speculatively, there is growing interest in (and controversy surrounding) the development of AI-empowered "emotion recognition" tools, raising the possibility that future tools could track patterns in judicial "tone" and perceived "emotional response".[40]

36 See, for example, Yan Campagnolo and Camille Andrzejewski, "The Most-Cited Law Review Articles of All Time by the Supreme Court of Canada" (2022) 60 Alta L Rev 129. See also Chapter 5.

37 See Veel and Glowach (this volume, Chapter 6).

38 See, for example, Lee Epstein, William M. Landes, and Richard A. Posner, "Inferring the Winning Party in the Supreme Court from the Pattern of Questioning at Oral Argument" (2010) 39 J of L Studies 433.

39 For a tool now available in Canada and its current deployment in relation to the Supreme Court of Canada, see Obiter.Ai's "Supreme (AI) Transcripts" project, online: https:// obiter.ai/blog/posts/2022-12-05-scc-transcripts/.

40 For an overview of these sorts of tools and a critical account of their limitations, see, for example, Kate Crawford, "Artificial Intelligence Is Misreading Emotions" *The Atlantic* (April 27, 2021).

Recusal motions are another area where analytics might be used.[41] Although parties bringing such motions face the "heavy burden" of displacing the "strong presumption of judicial impartiality" accorded to judges, the relevant test does not focus on proof of bias but rather on reasonable perceptions of bias.[42] What happens if a judicial analytics tool reports that a particular justice has a verifiable, pre-Supreme Court appointment, record of disproportionately disfavouring a certain type of litigant and this type of litigant is now a party before the Court? As Sean Rehaag observes, while "[c]ourts have regularly held that statistical differences in outcomes are not sufficient on their own to ground a finding of reasonable apprehension[,] ... [there are] exceptional circumstances where statistical evidence is so overwhelming that it meets the test for a reasonable apprehension of bias".[43] Even if such evidence were not admitted on a recusal motion, there could be negative impacts on public confidence in the Court if it were otherwise publicized.

Finally, there may be quasi-evidentiary uses for analytics data at the Supreme Court. Might lawyers attempt to bolster arguments about legal errors with analytics data showing that, in general, trial judges approach an issue differently than the trial judge did in the case before the Court? Lawyers could also seek to support arguments that the law should develop in a particular direction based on trends in Supreme Court case law or in lower court decisions, as revealed through analytics tools. Submissions containing impressionistic accounts of how the Court has historically approached an issue could be challenged with quantitative data produced by an analytics tool.

7.3.2.3 Benefits and Risks

As outlined above, judicial analytics tools can potentially offer limited strategic advantages to lawyers litigating a case before the Supreme Court. Such tools may also "open up" the development of the law insofar as they could reveal new litigation strategies or legal arguments.

However, the risks of inaccurate or misleading data are again a concern in this context. For example, if a lawyer argues, based on good faith but inaccurate data, that Justice X has a pattern of bias against accused persons who are Black, the public's perception of equality before the law could be unfairly but seriously damaged. On the flip side, overconfidence in data as necessarily disproving bias could lead to misleading and

---

41 McGill and Salyzyn, *supra* note 1 at 265–266.
42 Ibid.
43 Sean Rehaag, "Judicial Review of Refugee Determinations: The Luck of the Draw?" (2012) 38:1 Queen's LJ 1 at 34.

alienating claims about the fairness of the justice system. There are lots of ways in which bias exists in legal processes that cannot be captured in reported data points.

Separate concerns exist about the effects of judicial analytics tools on the development of the law. Data from judicial analytics tools could facilitate novel arguments, as noted above, but may also lead to the "flattening" of new legal developments. As litigants interact with the Court based only or primarily on what the Court has previously done, "feedback loops" could arise that make it less likely that litigants would advance creative or novel approaches to a legal problem, or make it harder for them to do so. In her examination of machine learning litigation prediction tools, Charlotte Alexander warns of the danger of the law becoming "endogenous and ossified".[44] This sort of danger is a particular concern at the level of the Supreme Court of Canada, where a core function of the Court is to ensure the law evolves appropriately.

The discussion in this section suggests another series of fundamental questions about the Supreme Court. Will current notions of judicial impartiality be sensible or sustainable in a future in which more detailed statistical information about judicial decision-making is available? Will we need a different doctrinal approach to recusals? To what degree should past practices guide the Court's future work?

7.3.3 Using Analytics to Assess the Work of the Supreme Court

As outlined above, litigators may be interested in tracking certain Court-level patterns as a means of seeking strategic advantages. The Court and the public may also be interested in this data in order to better understand what the Court is doing and to identify possible areas for improvement or further inquiry.

7.3.3.1 Using Analytics Data to (Self-)Assess the Work of the Court

In the previous section, we noted that statistical reports could reveal patterns in leave decisions and reliance on authorities. Court-level doctrinal trends and voting alignment patterns might also be captured by judicial analytics tools.[45] Additionally, analytics tools could deliver meta-analy-

---

44 Charlotte S. Alexander, "Litigation Outcome Prediction, Access to Justice, and Legal Endogeneity" in David Freeman Engstrom, ed., *Legal Tech and the Future of Civil Justice* (Cambridge: Cambridge University Press, 2023) at 170.

45 For an example of such statistics, see Mathen et al. (this volume, Chapter 4). See, also, "Scotus Statistics" *Harvard Law Review*, online: https://harvardlawreview.org/supreme -court-statistics.

ses of reasons, including data about readability (e.g. metrics related to reading level, length, and structure),[46] and could examine recordings of oral arguments for patterns in judicial questioning.[47] This sort of data could lead to a better understanding of the Court. It could also help prompt and inform reforms of the Court's practices.

A recent example of the use of statistics to reform court practices can be found in the United States: in response to a study concluding that the female justices of the Supreme Court of the United States were interrupted at disproportionate rates by their male colleagues and by male lawyers, the rules of oral argument were changed to allow each justice to ask questions individually after each lawyer's submissions are complete.[48]

7.3.3.2 Benefits and Risks

Using information from analytics tools to assess Court practices could advance rule of law values in several respects. First, increased access to data could lead to more transparency and accountability in the Court's work. Such data could facilitate improved insight into the Court's decision-making patterns and allow the public to advocate for, or the Court to implement, appropriate reforms. Again, the media might use analytics to enhance its reporting on the Court in order to better inform the public.[49] Second, judicial analytics can advance equality before the law, to the extent that it is used to identify and mitigate or correct biases against

---

46 For an example of this sort of analysis using analytics tools, see Mike Madden, "Stating It Simply: A Comparative Study of the Quantitative Readability of Apex Court Decisions from Australia, Canada, South Africa, the United Kingdom, and the United States" (2021) 23 NC J L & Tech 270. See, also, Nina Varsava, "Computational Legal Studies, Digital Humanities, and Textual Analysis" in Ryan Whalen, ed., *Computational Legal Studies* (Cheltenham: Edward Elgar Publishing, 2020).

47 For examples of this sort of analysis in the American context, see Jake S. Truscott and Adam Feldman, "The New Hot Bench: With Jackson Leading the Way, the Justices Are Speaking More during Oral Arguments" *SCOTUSblog.com* (December 30, 2022), online: https://www.scotusblog.com/2022/12/supreme-court-new-bench-with-ketanji-brown -jackson-justices-speaking-more-oral-arguments/, and Gregory M. Dickinson, "A Computational Analysis of Oral Argument in the Supreme Court" (2019) 28 Cornell J L & Pol'y 449. See, also, Terry Skolnik, "Hot Bench: A Theory of Appellate Adjudication" (2020) 61 BCL Rev 1271, for an account of the democratic and functionalist values of oral hearings and how such values may be enhanced or compromised by judicial behaviour at oral hearings.

48 See, for example, Adam Liptak, "Supreme Court Tries to Tame Unruly Oral Arguments" *The New York Times* (November 1, 2021). For the underlying studies, see Tonja Jacobi and Dylan Schweers, "Justice, Interrupted: The Effect of Gender, Ideology and Seniority at Supreme Court Oral Arguments" (2017) 103 Virginia L Rev 1379.

49 See, for example, Sean Fine, "Canada's Supreme Court Is Off-Balance as 'Large and Liberal' Consensus on the Charter Falls Apart" *The Globe and Mail* (January 15, 2022).

certain groups. Finally, the rule of law requires that the law be accessible, which means reasons for judgment must be intelligible and clear.[50] If analytics tools detect and highlight areas for improvement in the clarity of the Court's written judgments, this could increase the accessibility of the Court's written work.

However, there are challenges associated with using analytics tools to identify and isolate undesirable trends in the Court's work. Apparent associations may be too quickly or falsely overlaid with a causal interpretation that is not supported by the data. While the mantra, "correlation does not imply causation" is well known, "as humans, we cannot avoid thinking in terms of causality".[51] The context of the Supreme Court also raises special challenges. The Court's outputs – reasons for judgment – are highly constrained and shaped by the inputs that it receives.

Take, for example, a statistical account of what sources or authorities the Court tends to rely upon. In large part, when citing sources and authorities, the Court depends on those sources and authorities brought to its attention by the lawyers arguing the case. While the Court can do its own research, the scholarship or case law it cites also depends on the scholarship or case law that exists. So, while a statistical report might show that the Court cites more academic journal articles authored by men than women, this does not necessarily or automatically lead to the conclusion that the Court is biased against female academics. For any given case, one would need to know, among other things, the breakdown of the relevant articles by the genders of the authors, whether they are all equally available (i.e. some are available electronically while others are not), and which of the available articles were brought to the attention of the Court in written and oral submissions. There are often multiple, possibly contradictory, factors driving an observed data pattern. "Tidy" causal stories can be seductive but they are illusory in many cases.

On top of this, the risk of poor-quality tools producing bad data looms large and would be especially consequential if the Court were relying on that data to adjust its practices. The possible publication of "bad" data (or even the misinterpretation of accurate data) is particularly concerning in a judicial context, given that judges "are often prohibited by law or custom from defending themselves".[52]

Finally, there is a risk that the Supreme Court (or any court) might become too data-driven. In health care, for example, there is a growing

---

50 *R v Ferguson*, 2008 SCC at para. 68.
51 J.B. Asendorpf, "Bias Due to Controlling a Collider: A Potentially Important Issue for Personality Research" (2012) European Journal of Personality 26.
52 See, for example, Federation of Law Societies of Canada, *Model Code of Professional Conduct*, r. 5.6-1, Commentary [3].

"data overload" problem, whereby decision-makers have access to so much information, and are so overwhelmed by it, that the adoption of evidence-based practices is impeded.[53] For individual judges, information from judicial analytics tools could subtly (or unsubtly) create pressure to conform to, or align their behaviour with, perceived or explicitly introduced targets that flow from quantitative assessments.[54] Such pressures could quash diverse perspectives, and jeopardize the "structural impartiality" that facilitates sound judicial decision-making.[55] It will be critical for legal actors to be intentional and informed when engaging with – and especially when acting upon – analytics information.

Again, there are fundamental questions underpinning these issues. For example, when we collect information about the Supreme Court for the purposes of evaluation, what baselines or criteria are we measuring against? Which observed patterns should prompt reform and why? What are the limits to the empirical study of patterns in the Court's work?

7.4 Conclusion

In this chapter, we outlined some possible ways in which mainstreamed judicial analytics might impact the Supreme Court of Canada. In this conclusion, we identify four areas of concern going forward.

First, given the importance of accurate data about the Supreme Court, ensuring high-quality judicial analytics tools is paramount. For this reason, we have previously suggested that a "public model" be developed in Canada, whereby "a non-profit legal organization ... develop[s] high quality, free judicial analytics tools for public use".[56] Such a public model is advantageous as it "delinks quality assurance from commercial incentives and provides a free, trusted option that is available to everyone".[57]

Second, as outlined above, there is a risk that even the most accurate data about the Court will be misused or unfairly undermine public confidence in the Court if it is misinterpreted. Analytics information presented

---

53 See, for example, Deirdre E. Mylod and Thomas H. Lee, "Fixing Data Overload in Health Care" *Harvard Business Review* (March 16, 2022).

54 McGill and Salyzyn, *supra* note 1 at 271–272.

55 Sherrilyn A. Ifill, "Judging the Judges: Racial Diversity, Impartiality, and Representation on State Trial Courts" (1997) 39 BC L.Rev 95 at 119 explains, "[s]tructural impartiality is realized through the interaction of diverse viewpoints on the bench and the resulting decreased opportunity for one perspective to consistently dominate judicial decision-making". For discussion of this idea in the context of judicial diversity in Canada, see Sonia Lawrence, "Reflections: On Judicial Diversity and Judicial Independence" in Adam Dodek and Lorne Sossin, eds, *Judicial Independence in Context* (Toronto: Irwin Law, 2010) 193.

56 Ibid. at 280.

57 Ibid.

to the public must be properly contextualized, making data and statistical literacy a key skill for justice system stakeholders going forward.

Third, and relatedly, the Supreme Court and its justices will need to ensure that they understand judicial analytics tools and their outputs. Reports from judicial analytics tools are likely to play an increasingly significant role in how the public talks about, interacts with, and perceives the legitimacy of the Court. Information produced through analytics tools may even find its way into complaints against judges submitted to judicial regulators.[58] The Court and associated institutions and actors will have to be appropriately prepared to engage with this information.

Fourth, while analytics tools are new, envisioning their potential uses at the Supreme Court reinscribes decidedly old questions about the work of judging. Fundamental questions about judges and judging are intertwined with the gathering and evaluation of data about the Court and its judges (or potential judges). These questions underscore the importance of conducting analytics with a clear-eyed purpose and devoting careful attention to the relevant normative questions. As analyses of court data become easier to produce, issues of data overload, data misuse, and "data in the air" (i.e. collecting data without a purpose or baseline for evaluation) become significant risks. Such problems can frustrate the potential for analytics to add more transparency and accountability to the Court's work.

58 McGill and Salyzyn, *supra* note 1 at 281–282.

Index

For Product Safety Concerns and Information please contact our EU
representative GPSR@taylorandfrancis.com
Taylor & Francis Verlag GmbH, Kaufingerstraße 24, 80331 München, Germany